www.stressawarenessandprevention.com
www.thementalwellnessrevolution.com

Relieve Stress, Anxiety, Burnout, Panic Attacks & Agoraphobia The Same Way I Did

A Holistic Approach Featuring NLP, TFT, TFH,

New Age, Holistic & Mind Body Therapies

Written by

Suzanne J. Price

TFT (Tapping), EFT, NLP, TFH, Holistic Life & Personal Success Coach, Practitioner, Educator & Author

www.suzanneprice.com

www.stressawarenessandprevention.com
www.thementalwellnessrevolution.com

Relieve Stress, Anxiety, Burnout, Panic Attacks & Agoraphobia The Same Way I Did

A Holistic Approach Featuring NLP, TFT, TFH,

New Age, Holistic & Mind Body Therapies

Published by

Suzanne J. Price

All rights reserved. No part of this book may be used or reproduced in any manner whatsoever without prior written consent of the author.

Copyright © 2014 by Suzanne J. Price

ISBN: 978-0-9812862-5-9

Canadian Intellectual Property Certificate of Registration 2015

www.stressawarenessandprevention.com
www.thementalwellnessrevolution.com

The Bad News Is....

Stress Is Related To The Six Leading Causes Of Death

It Can and Does Manifest Into

Anxiety, Burnout, Panic Attacks and Agoraphobia

Stress Can Affect Absolutely Anyone &

It Often Seems To Strike Out Of The Blue

The Good News Is...

This Can Be Prevented & It Can Also Be Overcome

Learning How To Recognize The Symptoms And Manage The Stress In Your Life May Be One Of The Most Important Lessons You Could Ever Learn

www.suzanneprice.com

Relieve Stress, Anxiety, Burnout, Panic Attacks & Agoraphobia
The Same Way I Did

www.stressawarenessandprevention.com
www.thementalwellnessrevolution.com

A Word From The Author

Before you start reading this book I want you to know that I am not a doctor, counsellor or psychologist of any sort, nor do I work in the medical field. I am however someone, who suffered with every day stress that manifested into anxiety, panic attacks, burnout and agoraphobia. And, who after struggling with this condition for many years, found a way to overcome it, and get my life back.

In my efforts, besides training in the New Age, Alternative, Natural, and Mind Body Therapies, which ultimately helped me make a full recovery, I also developed a whole array of tools. These include an amazing stress awareness, prevention and management coaching program; several workshops which I teach live, online, and for corporations; The Stress & Burnout Awareness & Prevention series of books; a couple of campaigns, and of course my App called MY PANIC COACH. The stress related campaigns are: The Worldwide Stress & Burnout Awareness & Prevention Campaign, The Mental Wellness Revolution, and, The Student's Stress & Burnout Awareness & Prevention Campaign.

Relieve Stress, Anxiety, Burnout, Panic Attacks & Agoraphobia
The Same Way I Did

The ironic thing about me becoming what many now consider to be "an expert on stress" is the fact that not only had I never considered working in this field before. But I actually didn't even know what stress was until I moved to North America, as it was here that I first started to hear people from all walks of life, complain about being stressed. I was so unaware of what they were talking about that I actually had to ask around.

Also, even after I had recovered from my own ten year ordeal, and realized how my knowledge and experience had opened up an amazing career opportunity for me, I still resisted the field of stress management. Instead, I returned to another passion of mine which focussed more on personal and professional development.

In saying that, I have to admit that there was always something, niggling away in the back of my mind. It was that little voice (the one that was speaking for my conscience), that kept telling me that maybe I'd gone through this ordeal for a reason, and that perhaps this was my calling. And that considering I knew firsthand how debilitating these stress related conditions often are, and how difficult they can be to overcome, that maybe I should do something to help others.

I couldn't deny the fact that there were so few options available that offered any real help to those wanting to recover from these horrible conditions. I was also very aware that there were, and still are literally millions of people suffering. However, even though I knew full well what they were going through, the idea of me pursuing a career in this field was just too close for comfort. From my own standpoint, I knew that I needed to distance myself and rebuild my inner resources, and the only way to do that was to take a break from it altogether. Even so, as much as I tried to push those thoughts away, I knew that one day I'd probably share my story, if for no other reason, than to give those who suffer, some much needed hope.

However, even though I had decided to put all of this behind me for a while, there was something that really infuriated me, and that was the way that stress was often portrayed in the media. It seemed as though the emphasis of many of the reports was to exaggerate the statistics, as if to make us all believe that it is perfectly natural to be so stressed. Yet, while they keep regurgitating these stories, it seemed that no one was really telling us what to do to prevent it.

It was my frustration over this lack of information that inspired me to develop and launch The

www.stressawarenessandprevention.com
www.thementalwellnessrevolution.com

Worldwide Stress & Burnout Awareness & Prevention Campaign. My intention was purely to raise awareness for the purpose of prevention. So as part of this campaign I developed a very informative website, and wrote my first stress related book. It is called The Stress & Burnout Awareness & Prevention Guide. What started out as a tool to help people become aware of the symptoms and warning signs has now developed into the Stress & Burnout Awareness & Prevention series of books.

With that said, and although I have developed a whole series of stress less tools, my goal is to help people develop the skills to not only be able to handle life's stresses and challenges, but to ultimately live happier, healthier lives. There is a lot more to stress management than just trying to cope with, or manage stress. In fact, I truly believe that we need to reconsider what is really important in our lives, and to become more aware of the choices that we make. Ultimately we need to rethink how we can live, in a way that ensures that we have balance, and that we are living our lives on purpose. And that means learning how to effectively manage the various different aspects of our lives. My motto is that if we learn how to manage our lives then the stress will manage itself.

www.stressawarenessandprevention.com
www.thementalwellnessrevolution.com

This is why, that although I speak and write a lot about stress, especially from the perspective of awareness and prevention, the programs that I teach and write about are very holistic. They incorporate physical, mental, emotional, spiritual, social and environmental aspects of living, and I deliver these lessons through various media platforms.

To learn more about my upcoming programs, workshops, books, online products, and live events, please sign up for my newsletter on www.suzanneprice.com

How To Use This Book

This is the second book in my stress awareness, prevention and management series. The first one was written specifically to raise awareness for the purpose of prevention. It is full of ideas to help people become more aware of their own levels of stress in hopes that they can prevent it from manifesting into anxiety, burnout, panic attacks, depression or agoraphobia.

I then wrote this particular book to help those who suffer with such debilitating conditions. And in it I introduce the very same therapies I used to overcome 10 years of suffering from this, myself. With that said, there are some mind body exercises

www.stressawarenessandprevention.com
www.thementalwellnessrevolution.com

that may seem quite complex for the reader. They are actually quite easy to do, but since it may be easier for you to copy someone doing the exercises as opposed to reading the instructions while trying to do them, I have put some accompanying videos on a members section of my website www.suzanneprice.com

In order to get the most out of this book I'm going to suggest that you read it from cover to cover before attempting any of the exercises. Then when you are ready, simply follow the instructions or visit my website to follow along with the instructional videos.

If you have never worked with mind body therapies before, then you could be in for a pleasant surprise. I'd suggest that you keep an open mind while you explore the possibilities of what these New Age, Holistic, Alternative and Mind Body therapies can do for you.

Also while considering using these therapies, I'd like to bring to your attention the fact that many of them have been around for hundreds, if not thousands of years. Some have been, and still are held in such high regard that they may be integrated into daily life. This is true in many parts of the world, and has been the case, probably since the beginning of time.

In saying this, I want you to know that I am not suggesting that you use these or any other therapies instead of, or as a substitute to taking the advice of your doctor or health care provider. I am however suggesting that you do have a choice, and that there are several options available. If you chose to follow any of the advice, or participate in any of the exercises I speak about or write about in this book, please be advised that you are doing so at your own risk.

To learn more about my other personal and professional development projects, please visit one of the websites listed below. On the sites you will also be able to download some free gifts, and sign up for my monthly newsletter.

www.suzanneprice.com

www.stressawarenessandprevention.com

www.thementalwellnessrevolution.com

www.stressawarenessandprevention.com
www.thementalwellnessrevolution.com

Other Books & Programs Written By Suzanne J. Price

- ♥ The Stress & Burnout Awareness & Prevention Guide
- ♥ The Students Stress & Burnout Awareness & Prevention Guide
- ♥ It's Your Life – So What Are You Going To Do With It?
- ♥ New Year Resolutions, Goals, Dreams & Aspirations
- ♥ How To Turn That First Glance Into A Date.
- ♥ Tapping Into Your Mind Body Magic

Workshops & Programs Include:

- ♥ Tapping Into Your Mind Body Magic
- ♥ Take Control Of Panic Attacks The Same Way I Did

APPS

- ♥ My Panic Coach

To learn about upcoming product launches and book releases be sure to visit my site and grab your free eBook. We will then keep you posted on upcoming events.

www.stressawarenessandprevention.com
www.thementalwellnessrevolution.com

Table Of Contents

My Story - *page 15*

The Diagnosis That Turned A Panic Attack Into A Panic Disorder - *page 23*

Seeking Help And Hoping For A Recovery - *page 31*

Searching For A Cure And Taking A New Approach *page 43*

Making Sense Of The Horrible Symptoms Of Stress, Anxiety, Panic Attacks, Burnout & Agoraphobia – *page 53*

The Stress Less Approach To Conquering Your Stress, Anxiety, Panic Attacks, Burnout And Agoraphobia – *page 73*

Learn To Identify Exactly Where Your Stress Is Coming From – *page 109*

Reinvent Yourself To Become A More Confident And Empowered Version Of You – *page 123*

Relieve Stress, Anxiety, Burnout, Panic Attacks & Agoraphobia The Same Way I Did

www.stressawarenessandprevention.com
www.thementalwellnessrevolution.com

Disclaimer

While reading this book please keep in mind that I am not a trained medical professional nor do I claim to be one. I am in no way suggesting that you use the materials in this book as a substitute for professional help.

I am however someone who has suffered with stress which manifested into burnout, anxiety, panic attacks and agoraphobia which affected every aspect of my life for ten years. However upon finding the right therapies and applying them to the different aspects of my life I fully recovered from these debilitating disorders.

My intentions with this book is to provide you with some general information and guidance as to how alternative therapies combined with lifestyle changes could possibly help you overcome stress, anxiety, panic attacks, burnout or agoraphobia.

www.stressawarenessandprevention.com
www.thementalwellnessrevolution.com

Got Panic Attacks?

Well Now There's An App For That

My Panic Coach App

The Main Feature Of This App Is The Panic Button. When Pressed A Calming Voice Will Talk You Through A Panic Attack In Real Time

These Exercises Have Been Proven To Help Lead A Person Out Of A State Of Stress & Into One Of Calm & Relaxation. And To Feel More Centered, Balanced, Connected, Grounded & Calm

To learn more please visit

www.suzanneprice.com

www.mypaniccoach.com

Relieve Stress, Anxiety, Burnout, Panic Attacks & Agoraphobia The Same Way I Did

www.stressawarenessandprevention.com
www.thementalwellnessrevolution.com

My Story

If you had known me before I suffered with anxiety, panic attacks, burnout and agoraphobia, you never in a million years would have imagined someone like me, suffering with something as debilitating as this.

I was an easy going, happy-go-lucky, fun loving person who took everything in stride. Not too much ever bothered me, and when something did, I'd simply go for a walk, think things through, and find a solution to my problem.

I certainly wasn't someone who suffered with stress, nor was I the typical candidate to do so. For the most part I was happy, confident and outgoing. I was close to my family and friends and had no problem striking up a conversation with anyone I'd meet. I enjoyed the outdoors, horse riding, skiing and boating. I spent plenty of time in nature, and hiked and walked for several miles a day. I had what most people would consider a pretty well balanced life.

Knowing this, you would then have to wonder why, or how, someone like me could have possibly ended up suffering with something as debilitating as this. And although this condition seemed to come on out of the blue, the worst part of it was that no matter what I tried, I just couldn't seem to get over it. The result being that I ended up suffering with this debilitating disorder for about ten years?

The Bad News Is

Stress Can And Does Manifest Into

Anxiety, Panic Attacks, Burnout And Agoraphobia

This Can Happen To Absolutely Anyone And It Often Seems To Strike Out Of The Blue

This Happened To Me, And It Could Also Happen To You....

The Good News Is

With The Right Awareness This Can Be Prevented

And With The Right Tools It Can Also Be Overcome

My First Symptoms

I first realized that something was wrong when I started to experience dizzy spells, as well as the discomfort that many describe as being dissociated, disconnected, bewildered, or unreal. Since I'd never experienced anything like this before, and because this was only happening at work I wondered if I might have been allergic to something in my work place. Then one day, as if right out of the blue I suffered a full blown panic attack. It was a terrifying experience which caught me completely off guard. And by the time it was over I felt so exhausted that I could barely stop myself from dropping to the floor.

As with most panic attacks the experience brought on a great sense of urgency, and a need to escape. So I immediately left work to go home, only I suffered a second attack within minutes of getting in my car. Little did I know at the time, these two panic attacks were the first of many that I was about to suffer. Not to mention that they were also about to change my entire life.

A Typical Panic Attack For Me

My panic attacks would come on so quickly, in an instant actually, and no sooner did I feel the first symptom and it would turn into a full blown attack. This would happen within seconds, and once started there was no turning back, or stopping it until it had run its course.

For me I would usually notice getting really hot, especially around my face, neck and ears. Then within moments I'd break into a sweat and start trembling all over. My heart would race like crazy and my body would become so tense that I could feel myself trembling on the insides as well as out.

It would then seem as though all of my senses would become heightened for a moment, but then they would almost fade out, leaving me feeling disconnected and numb. This meant that my hearing would become hypersensitive and then I'd get a high pitched ringing in my ears, making it difficult to hear anything else at all. My eyesight would also become very dim or blurred to the point that it seemed as though I was losing my sight.

My mouth would also dry out and the tightening in my throat made it difficult to swallow. There were so many symptoms that I'd feel as though I couldn't get a grip on this thing at all. It would seem as though everything became speeded up to the point that I'd want to run and hide. But my shaky legs would become so numb that they'd feel as though they had turned to lead. Finally, I'd reach a point where I could hardly move at all, as panic attacks are usually so violent on a person's body that they can literally leave the victim paralyzed by fear.

During an attack you experience so many symptoms and sensations that happen more or less at once. Yet for me the feeling of disconnect and dissociation would cause me to feel as though I was no longer experiencing anything through my senses at all. It was so overwhelming that I would feel as though I was fading out, or that I was going to disappear. A sensation that most would find difficult to even imagine, unless that is they have ever experienced anything like this for themselves.

Thankfully an attack only ever lasted a matter of minutes because any longer and I probably would have passed out. It's almost as if you are literally being taken to the brink of death. As if someone is holding you over the edge of a cliff and threatening to let you go, and you are so terrified that you are pleading for it to stop. Then, as if it was some sick or cruel joke you'd get pulled back to safety, and just like that, the overwhelming feelings of panic would stop. It's that terrifying.

The whole thing is so crazy, and encompasses your body mind and soul. But luckily, your body cannot maintain all this craziness for too long so it suddenly just stops. It is over in a matter of minutes, quite quickly really. Although it feels like forever when you are having one, as they certainly last long enough to cause one to wonder if they will actually survive at all.

No wonder so many people who suffer with panic attacks actually think they are going to die, as while you are in the middle of one it certainly feels that way.

The Intensity Of My Panic Attacks

Were Debilitating To Say The Very Least.

My drive home from work was unbearable. I was still shaken up and felt so exhausted that I thought I was going to have to pull over and leave my car. I felt as though I wanted to crawl into a cave, and although I knew I didn't have far to go, the mere sight of a stop sign or thought of a traffic light turning red, sent surges of fear and panic through my body.

Needless to say the feelings of overwhelm made it very difficult for me to concentrate on my driving, and the numbness caused me to feel as though I was going to pass out. Luckily I must have been running on autopilot as I did make it home in one piece. Then as I stepped inside the house, locked the door behind me, and sank down into my couch I felt a sense of relief. The numbness started to fade and I could feel my body coming back to life. Although my mind was still scrambling to make sense of it all.

As I sat watching the television in an effort to distract myself all sorts of thoughts rushed through my mind. I was still feeling awful, bewildered and exhausted. And even though I was now in the safety of my home I still felt tense and anxious. My head felt as though it was disconnected from my body. I felt so out of sorts that every time I made a sudden move, or attempted to get up off the couch, I'd come over feeling so dizzy that I'd have to hold on to something to prevent myself from falling.

I suspected that I'd suffered a panic attack, or two of them including the one in the car, as I had experienced them before. Although this time there were some obvious differences. Those being that on the two occasions I'd had a panic attack before, they had been isolated incidents. Also, both had been a result of some extremely anxiety provoking situations that I'd been dealing with at the time they had occurred. However this time I really couldn't put my finger on anything that had been particularly stressful. Nor could I imagine what might have triggered them.

To make matters worse, I had never heard of anything like this before. And since there was no apparent reason for this sudden onset of panic and the confusion that accompanied it, I became extremely worried. Not to mention the fact that I was now also terrified that it might happen again.

Needless to say I had all sorts of thoughts running through my mind. I didn't know what I was suffering with, or what to expect next. As I sat there thinking about the feelings in my head I started to wonder if I could have been suffering with some sort of mental illness. And I was concerned about whether or not this was something that I'd be able to overcome. I had so many unanswered questions, including, would they or could they actually lock someone up for suffering with something as strange as this.

All of this uncertainty stirred up more feelings of fear and concern. So much so that I wasn't even sure if I should risk going to see a doctor, or wait it out and hope this thing would just go away by its self. However, by that evening I had worked myself up into such a state that the condition had worsened. Now, realizing how quickly this had come on, and worried that it could potentially get worse, I decided to take a chance and immediately sought medical advice.

The Diagnosis That Turned A Panic Attack Into A Panic Disorder

That night, I went to a walk in clinic where I was seen by a very professional looking male physician. I was feeling very anxious and also scared about what I was about to hear. Still visibly trembling and somewhat emotional, I felt stupid for not being able to pull myself together and just get over this.

As I spoke the doctor just stood there looking at me with a very stern look on his face. I told him about the dizzy spells and feelings of bewilderment, and described the symptoms of the panic attacks. Then when my three minutes were up and I stopped to take a deep breath, he didn't hesitate to jump right in with his diagnosis. He quickly scribbled a note on his prescription pad, and as he tore it off and handed it to me he abruptly announced, "Your Pregnant!" Then with no further discussion he turned around and walked right back out through the door.

For a brief moment I felt a sense of relief as I had not been diagnosed with an incurable disease, nor had I been committed to an asylum. However, since this doctor's diagnosis was the most ridiculous thing I'd ever heard, I left his office feeling none the wiser. And while still a little stunned by his response, I drove away wondering if I could have been suffering with something so out of the ordinary that he simply didn't know what it was. And if this was the case then maybe there was no known cure for it either. This also meant that I still didn't know what to expect next, or what to do to overcome this. And to make matters worse I wondered if it could even get worse.

By the way, the prescription which this doctor gave me was for anti anxiety and anti depressant medications. To this day, I still haven't figured out if the drugs were supposed to have been for me, or if they were meant for the baby. And in case you are wondering, no, I was not pregnant.

From what I remember I went back to work the following day where I felt even more bewildered and anxious. I was desperate to find answers and wanted these feelings to be gone, so I left work and drove myself straight to see another doctor.

This time I saw a female doctor. After I described my symptoms and told her about the experience I'd had the day before, she quickly pointed out that it was stress. However, even though she was very matter of fact, she didn't offer any further explanation.

Also, since I couldn't understand how something like stress could have possibly generated so many horrible physical symptoms, I didn't find her diagnosis very convincing. I sat there wondering if she had really understood what I'd been trying to tell her, as for me to have been able to accept this diagnosis I needed to understand what was really going on. And that meant that I needed an explanation as to what had caused the symptoms. Why it had came on so suddenly, and how long it was going to last. I also wanted to know what I needed to do in order to get rid of it. But with no further explanation she simply escorted me to the door, told me to take a few days off work, and handed me another prescription.

I did take a few days off but found it very difficult to relax. However, I recognized that the symptoms had been more aggravated whenever I was at work and was dreading having to go back. Still, determined to get to the bottom of whatever this was, and to get rid of the symptoms, I decided to see yet another doctor.

Doctors number three and four responded to my concerns in exactly the same way, although one guy actually made a bit of a joke about me having the shakes. His light heartedness did help me breathe a little easier as I thought surely he wouldn't have made a joke about my condition, if he had thought it was something really serious. However, since I still hadn't heard any sort of explanation of why I was feeling this way, I became even more worried. I did however walk away from both of these doctors with additional prescriptions to get even more antidepressants, and anti-anxiety pills.

By now I was getting very good at walking into doctor's offices, explaining my symptoms and grilling them with questions. I also had enough prescriptions to have started my own little drug company. However, there was no way that I was going to take this medication until someone explained what it was for, or how it was going to help me. I didn't understand how I could have even been stressed never mind how these physical symptoms could have possibly been caused by anything that was going on in my life.

It seemed as though the doctors I'd seen didn't have an explanation as to what I was going through. Nor did they understand the importance of me knowing what this was, or why I was now suffering with it. This gave me even more to worry about as I thought if none of the doctors really knew what this was. Then how were they possibly going to be able to help me?

Even though I'd taken a few days off work I still wasn't feeling any relief. I was dreading the thought of having to go back, and I had no idea if, or what I should tell my employers. I was also aware that the powers that be were more concerned about me not being available to run their business than they were about me or my health. So to avoid any additional stress which would have been brought on as a result of me taking more sick time, I quit my job as it seemed as though that was the only way I'd be able to get well. I gave myself two weeks off to recuperate, thinking this would've been plenty of time to get well, but as I soon found out this was not going to be the case at all.

By the end of the two weeks I still wasn't feeling any better. I hadn't been able to sleep, and was feeling anxious all of the time. I was also having several panic attacks a day. And I felt so dissociated and disconnected that I'd become all but confined to my home. Since I'd not seen any improvement at all I was also starting to worry about, if it was even possible for me to get well again. And this became compounded by the fact that I now also had to consider how I was going to manage financially.

By now I'd been suffering with this condition for about two weeks, yet so much of my life had changed. I'd had to quit my job because I just couldn't function at work. I was turning down all sorts of social invitations and avoiding everyone, as I didn't know what to tell them or how to explain what I was going through. I couldn't drive, and I couldn't even get the mail from outside my front door without having another attack or literally becoming paralyzed by fear. And the scariest part about all of this was, because I still didn't know how or why this had happened. I wasn't even sure if I was going to be able to change my life back again. And if it was going to be possible, then how was I going to do it.

This was all very frustrating. I was still so stressed and burnt out that I was constantly anxious, drained and frazzled, and was experiencing the dizziness and feelings of numbness most of the time. I couldn't eat or sleep properly, and was suffering with panic attacks on a daily basis. I had also reached a point where I couldn't even leave my house alone. This was all so bizarre and yet I couldn't see any end in sight. It was affecting every single area of my life to the point that I, as well as my life had changed so much that not even I could recognize myself.

By this time I had visited four different doctors yet still had not heard any sort of explanation as to why this had happened, what was going on with me, or why I was suffering with all of these symptoms. I did not know what to expect next, or what to do to overcome this. I was walking around with two bottles of pills in my purse and a pile of prescriptions that I hadn't even had filled. And the worst thing about it was that I wasn't even sure if it was possible to get over this. The difficulty I'd experienced while trying to get my questions answered only added to my concerns. And the feeling of being kept in the dark exacerbated the whole problem.

www.stressawarenessandprevention.com
www.thementalwellnessrevolution.com

Seeking Help And Hoping For A Recovery

As time went on I became more and more desperate. I was determined to get well so decided to take things into my own hands. Being a big believer that the right knowledge is power, I set out to learn everything I could about the subject. We didn't have internet at the time so my first plan of action was to visit the UBC bookstore, where I bought every book that I could find on the subject. These were not just your typical self help books, as they were the same books used by students training in the mental health field.

Many of the original books on the subject had been written by western trained counsellors, psychologists or psychiatrists. This meant that most of them seemed to say pretty much the same thing, and included the doom and gloom about what they deem as "mental disorders". They of course also supported the notion that people needed therapy and/or medication in order to manage this, which of course is a typical westernized response. They also reported on the ever popular statistics which are used to emphasis the enormity of the problem.

Most of the books also included questionnaires or inventories which readers are encouraged to fill out. One good thing about these tools is that they give a person the opportunity to determine what he/she may be suffering with, or at least according to the questionnaires. The bad thing about them is that just about anyone could identify with almost any of the symptoms. This means that practically any willing participant could end up diagnosing themselves, or being diagnosed as having just about any mental or emotional disorder under the sun.

Another thing I personally don't like about these diagnostic tools is that they often delve into yours, as well as your family's personal history. The problem with this is that it is very difficult to resist the temptation of wanting to diagnose everyone else in your family too. And when you do this it can be very easy to buy into the idea that whatever you are suffering with could be hereditary. This idea in itself can then become a huge obstacle to getting well. Especially as most people, including many doctors, have bought into the idea that if you are suffering with something that is hereditary, then it is not going to be possible to overcome it. Not only is this not necessarily true, but such a diagnosis, or assumption could become one of the biggest obstacles to recovery.

When a person is suffering from something like this, they need hope that they can recover, and they need as many options as possible. Telling people that they can't get well because they have a genetic problem, or that they are suffering with something that is hereditary, tends to take that hope, and any possible choices away. Not to mention the fact that such news could leave a sufferer feeling doomed, and this will likely only add to the problem.

However, after reading these books I was able to gain a better understanding of what I was suffering with. I also decided to take the advice of the authors, and that was to seek out the help of a therapist. Now armed with this new knowledge I started calling around to find someone who could help me, but most of the therapists I talked to admitted that they didn't deal with this issue. However, when I finally found someone who was up for the challenge, I was relieved to be able to book an appointment.

Even so, I was still feeling anxious all of the time. I felt defeated, and I desperately wanted to get well. I wanted my life back, and after reading those books I thought for sure that the answer to my prayers was to go to therapy.

When I arrived at the therapist's office I told her what I'd been going through. I was expecting her to explain what this horrendous condition was and why I was now suffering with it, or to at least help me figure it out. However she did no such thing, but instead after hearing me out the therapist had me sit quietly in a chair and perform an exercise. I had to recite 5 things I could feel, 5 things I could hear, and 5 things I could see. Assuming she knew what she was doing I refrained from asking why and simply did what I had been instructed to do.

For my homework the therapist suggested that I wear an elastic band around my wrist, and snap it against my skin if I felt anxious. This was supposed to distract me or help me "snap" out of it. Thinking I would just trust the process I left the session, still feeling disappointed and a little confused. I then anxiously waited until I saw her again, hoping that we'd get around to talking more about this condition and figure out a way to overcome it.

The following week I went back to see the same therapist only to go through pretty much the same process. The focus of the session revolved around the chair exercise again. I kept telling her how desperate I was to get well, and how all I wanted was to have my life back. I repeatedly asked her to explain what this was and why I was now suffering with it. But she just kept ignoring my questions.

Instead she told me that I just needed to start doing whatever it was that I liked to do, and as I got used to doing it the anxiety should hopefully subside. Her response seemed ridiculous, especially as I had been doing the very things that I loved to do right up until I started suffering with the anxiety. She had no response to me telling her this either, so I was starting to wonder if she had any idea about what it was that I was going through. Or if she was going to be able to help me.

I went to a few more sessions expecting that at some point she would have something worthwhile to say, but nothing was changing at all. Finally one day I arrived at her office in tears. Time was going on and I wasn't getting any better, in fact I was feeling worse. I'd been doing everything that she had been telling me to do even though I was completely frustrated by the fact that she had not addressed my questions or concerns. She still hadn't explained anything about this condition nor had we explored why I was suffering with it now. We hadn't even discussed what was going on in my life.

When it came time for her to instruct me to do the chair exercise again, I finally asked her why. Then, jokingly commented that I thought we had determined that I wasn't deaf, dumb or blind during the first session that I'd done this.

For the last time I asked her to explain this to me, and reiterated how desperate I was to get well. She paused for a moment and then quietly asked if I had considered whether or not my symptoms were caused by my own anxiety, or if it was someone else's. Needless to say, that was the last time I saw that particular therapist.

Over the following months I saw several others, who sadly all approached my concerns in a similar manner, and who were all telling me exactly the same thing. And that was that this was just a part of who I was, and that I should just accept it. I kept telling them that I thought that was the most ridiculous thing I'd heard, and questioned how it could've possibly been part of who I was when I hadn't had it before. I was also abundantly clear that I didn't want to be suffering with this now either, and that I would've done anything to get rid of it. All I needed was for someone to tell me how.

Other than adding a couple more useless exercises such as imagining a stop sign, or saying the words "relax or peace" whenever I started to feel anxious or panicky, none of these people seemed to have a clue about how to help me. They just kept telling me to go and do whatever I wanted to do and one day I should get used to doing it. Then, with any luck the anxiety should hopefully just subside.

There had been a popular book out at the time written by a doctor whose message was pretty much what these therapists had been repeating. And although the advice may have been helpful for someone who was hesitant to take a chance, or even a little afraid, it certainly was not relevant for anyone suffering with something as crippling this. Being, anxiety, panic attacks, depression or agoraphobia.

The more I heard this sort of feedback the more convinced I became that none of these therapists had a clue about what I was suffering with. They obviously had no idea of how awful it felt, or how incapacitating anxiety and panic attacks are. And the only thing I now knew for sure was that none of these particular therapists had any idea of how they could help me get well.

The thing about anxiety and panic attacks is that the symptoms can become so debilitating, that they have the power to prevent a sufferer from doing the very things they absolutely love to do. This can literally bring a person's life to a standstill, with some people even becoming housebound. And even though most sufferers desperately want nothing more than to just be able to go for a walk, have coffee with a friend, or get at least some resemblance of their old life back. It can seem all but impossible to do.

If you need further convincing about how debilitating these conditions can be then image this. I have read about, and have had some people tell me that they have been so anxious on occasion, that they too had literally become paralyzed by fear. In fact, many of these people also believe that had something tragic happened to one of their children, where they needed to get the child to the hospital, they simply would not be able to leave their home to take them. As someone who has had firsthand experience of how crippling this can be, even though I do not have children I can certainly relate to this. The intensity of this fear is so overwhelming and it affects men in just the same way as it does women.

What this means is that in order for a person to be able to go out and do the very things that they would love to do, they need to be able to get rid of the horrendous symptoms first. And this is an issue that a lot of therapists can't seem to get their heads around. The reason being that while talk therapy is used to deal with thoughts and words, and is often intended to get people to change their "minds" about things. It is not usually powerful enough, or at least not as a standalone, to help sufferers relieve their intense symptoms of anxiety, panic attacks, depression or agoraphobia.

The final therapist I saw sat me on a chair in the middle of the room. He then observed me as he talked to (my now ex), and entertained himself by playing with his beard. After about fifteen minutes, when he first acknowledged me even being in the room, he asked me if I felt as though I was the center of attention. Then when my ex piped up and said that I loved to have fun and always seemed to see the funny side of things. The therapist responded by saying that this was probably part of my problem. I just wasn't taking life seriously enough. *Amazing*! And we wonder why we have so many people being diagnosed as being mentally ill in this part of the world!

Looking back I often wonder if this guy might have actually been a patient who'd escaped from a mental asylum, locked the real therapist up in the closet and then proceeded to play therapist for the day. This would be the only plausible reason for this person's odd behaviour. Sadly I didn't think about this before I paid the idiot.

By now I was completely convinced that not only was I wasting my time, but the therapists seemed to be getting more out of the sessions than I was. Maybe I was the one who should have been getting paid for my time and expertise. I was frustrated and I just didn't know where to turn to next. I became even more desperate as it seemed that my options were running out.

I was starting to wonder if I was ever going to be able to get well again or if I was going to be stuck with this condition forever. In saying this, I want you to know that there are some very good therapists around, but you do need to know what you are looking for and how to find one who can help you. Otherwise you could end up wasting no end of money and suffer needlessly in the meantime.

At this point in time it was probably going on two years since I had suffered that first panic attack. I felt as though I'd tried everything, and had resigned myself to the fact that I'd probably never get over this. I had also come to the conclusion that I may never work outside the home again, and I needed to find a way to make some money.

My determination was being stomped down by the lack of progress. I felt defeated and doomed, and my disappointment was causing me to feel more depressed. I felt like a prisoner in my own home and I could see no way out. I still couldn't drive or go anywhere alone, and I was very anxious even when out with family.

Some days were better than others, but even on the good ones I'd spend hours psyching myself up to get out of the house. On the odd occasions that I'd succeed I typically couldn't go too far, often only managing to walk as far as the neighbour's, or two or three houses down the road. However, even then it wasn't uncommon for me to turn around and become so panicked that I'd barely be able to make it back home again.

Between all of the reading I'd done, the therapy sessions I had gone to, and the months of trying to get well, I figured a few things out on my own. I had definitely figured out what was not working for me, and decided that I needed to find a new approach.

I had also come to the conclusion that there are many different aspects of stress, and that each one needed to be dealt with differently. But perhaps most importantly, I'd realized that most of the symptoms were physical. And this meant that whatever I was suffering with was in fact a mind body experience. Maybe, this condition which is now more often referred to as a "mental illness" is not "all in the head" after all. No wonder the talk therapy hadn't been working for me, finally things were starting to make sense.

Searching For A Cure And Taking A New Approach

Up until this point I had felt really misunderstood, I was trying to get rid of the worrisome symptoms and yet nobody was even acknowledging my concerns. It seemed as though my physical symptoms were simply being overlooked or ignored because we were talking in different languages. I was talking about symptoms, sensations and feelings, and the therapists were talking about thoughts and words. I now knew that what I was dealing with was a mind body experience and that I needed to find another way. And that meant that I needed to learn about the mind body system, and in particular how its connection was affected by stress. This realization inspired me to explore the world of mind body therapies.

Now I was even more determined to get well and felt that I might have been onto something. With this new insight I started researching mind body therapies and I looked for the best methods to train in. This was all very new to me, but I dove right in and started training in One Brain Learning Awareness and NLP.

Both therapies proved to offer amazing tools which could help people in so many areas of their life, but I still wasn't clear about how they could help me overcome my anxiety. I was also still actively looking for help, and as luck would have it I came across a doctor who referred to himself as, a recovering psychologist. His self proclaimed title was a result of him now practicing New Age and alternative therapies and getting some excellent results. By this time I was willing to try anything so I thought that I'd give him a try.

During our first visit we talked briefly about what I'd been through. He then told me about a relatively new therapy and asked if I'd be willing to give it a try. Upon my approval, the doctor then explained what we were going to do.

He then showed me how he would use muscle testing to determine where in the mind body system the stress had caused disruptions. Then, upon determining the correct treatment points, led me through a series of tapping, eye movements, humming and counting. This was such an easy process that it seemed kind of childlike, and as I followed his lead we performed what seemed like one of the most ridiculous things I'd ever done. At this point I was still wondering if he might have been joking around. But since he was so sweet I decided to just play along as I didn't want to offend him.

The therapy, which is called Thought Field Therapy, uses muscle testing to identify any possible issues within the energy system of the body. This in itself is a very different approach to the typical gathering of verbal information, or having a client fill out a questionnaire, a common method that is used by most therapists. Muscle Testing is very easy, painless and personalized, as well as accurate. But perhaps the most fascinating thing about this method is that it literally overrides whatever you are thinking. And instead gathers information directly from the source of the stress, with that being stored in the mind body system. Perhaps one of the reasons that it is so effective is because it keeps the analytical brain out of the way, which in reality is the complete opposite to talk therapy.

After determining which points I needed to activate the doctor then walked me through the corrective process, using muscle testing to check for progress as we went along. By the time the session had come to an end I was feeling more relaxed, but I assumed that was because I felt comfortable with this particular person. I was relieved to have finally found someone who seemed to understand what I was going through and who genuinely had my interests at heart.

As I got ready to leave his office I was expecting the anxiety to well up again, but thankfully that never happened. So, I walked down the stairs and stepped out onto the street. I still couldn't believe how different I felt compared to just an hour earlier, and I was dying to go for a walk. As I looked to the right I could see the North Shore Mountains in the distance and felt inspired to walk all of the way there. Wanting to test this out, I turned and started walking towards the mountains. I felt completely at ease and amazed that I was no longer feeling anxious. I could hardly believe that I was seriously considering walking home.

However as I approached the corner at the end of the block, a familiar little voice piped up to remind me to be careful. It was telling me not to forget that if I went too far I might have another panic attack. And if that happened then I might not be able to get back to the car. This was not what I wanted to hear. However, since I was so aware of how panic attacks can suddenly strike out of the blue, and how they can literally bring a person to their knees, I hesitated. And as I stood there looking at the mountains I became aware of the internal conflict in my mind.

I truly believed that I could've made it home, in fact I felt so good I probably could have ran there. But that little voice became even more persistent, and it persuaded me to give in by rationalizing that maybe I should test this out when I was closer to home. Reluctantly I turned around and hesitantly walked back to my car.

I remember feeling so disappointed. I had always loved to go walking and used to walk everywhere before I suffered with this, but that had all come to an end. Because I'd suffered with panic attacks and agoraphobia for so long I now had the evidence of what could happen if I wasn't careful. And since it had prevented me from living my life for so long, I was very aware of the power it could have over me.

Herein lays another huge problem when you suffer with anxiety, panic attacks and agoraphobia, or any fears for that matter. In order to avoid the possibility of having another debilitating attack, we set limits for ourselves. These limits are usually formed around our capabilities, in other words, what we think we can, or cannot do. Then we stay within those limits to protect ourselves from the incredible pain and discomfort that we could easily encounter again if we were to push ourselves too far. Or venture into what we now believe to be the perceived danger zones.

We then take these limits on as a new truth and they become installed in our subconscious minds. Now, locked into the mind body system, they have the power to reinforce any limiting and negative beliefs we may already have about ourselves.

In the process these beliefs become part of our identity and this is one of the ways that we unconsciously reinvent ourselves. Sadly we often commit to these new beliefs and this puts us at risk of spending the rest of our lives living within the boundaries of our own minds.

I was so disappointed to have given in to that little voice but I now knew there was hope. I was determined that I was going to get over this. And even though I felt as though I'd made a deal with the devil by agreeing to trade in my freedom just to have the ability to go for a little walk, I was now no longer willing to compromise in such a way.

I'd put so much work into trying to get well, but I was still becoming even more determined to get my life back. In fact, I had reached a point where I was no longer willing to accept putting up with the limits that had been holding me back. Now I wanted even more. I wanted to become more confident, more empowered and more courageous. I wanted to set myself free and to become stronger than I had ever been in the past.

There had always been things that I avoided because I was too afraid to do them. They may have seemed insignificant but they certainly had the power to hold me back, and prevent me from living my life to the fullest. I had been hesitating in life and had stood back so many times when I desperately wanted to speak up, or participate. But now I was no longer willing to do that. I wasn't willing to buy into the idea that I wasn't going to get well, nor was I willing to compromise. I had reached a point where I decided that not only was I going to completely get over this, but I was also determined to become unstoppable!

By now I had learned a lot about anxiety, panic attacks and agoraphobia. I knew what it felt like to live with this and I knew how it could negatively impact any area of a person's life. But more importantly I had started to realize that there are actually many aspects of this condition, with one being that this is in fact a mind body experience. I'd also had a few positive experiences with mind body therapies, and was starting to see how they may be the answer to me getting my life back. Now all I needed to do was to figure out which therapies were going to be the most powerful and learn all that I could. I needed to find a way to outsmart this stress, and the positive experience I'd had, inspired me once again to keep on searching.

As luck would have it there was going to be a Thought Field Therapy training in Vancouver that following week so I, along with my sister signed up to take the course. We first took the weekend intensive where we learned the fundamentals and then went on to take the advanced training before repeating it all again. Fourteen years later I still take any training I can as there are always new discoveries of how these amazing therapies can help people in so many areas of their life.

I have to say that I'm a huge fan of TFT because not only have I taken extensive training in it, experimented with it, and practiced it for so many years, but I've also experienced its power firsthand. I know from my own experience that this is one of the most powerful tools I've ever used, and it definitely played a role in helping me overcome my own relentless anxiety, panic attacks and agoraphobia.

When I first started training in the various therapies I found myself in the same position as so many other practitioners who simply don't know how, or where to apply some of these tools. But since I was on a mission to combat my own very specific problem I was able to easily identify which exercises would work on which aspects of the stress. For this reason my anxiety and panic attacks were now working to my advantage. Not only was I able to experiment on my own issues but I was also able to figure out what was, or was not going to be able to help.

The more I learned about and experienced New Age and Alternative Therapies the more fascinated and impressed I became. I trained in as many of the therapies as I could. And after experimenting with different modalities I found a few that if applied in the right way, were powerful enough to help combat this type of stress. My top picks are TFT, NLP, One Brain, TFH and Bach Remedies. All of which work on the mind body system, or energy level, while bypassing the analytical mind which has the ability to easily outsmart almost any form of talk therapy.

Over the years and through my training I've experimented from the position of both client and practitioner, and I finally figured out how to get well. And in the process I've been able to completely annihilate my own horrible anxiety which had held me hostage for years. On my

www.stressawarenessandprevention.com
www.thementalwellnessrevolution.com

journey to wellness I've also become so much more confident than I'd ever been before. I'm now also spending my life working with all of the things I feel so passionate about, and living my life to the fullest.

At this point I still use all of these therapies in my personal and professional life. I've incorporated them into my coaching sessions, workshops and programs. And teach and write about them in my books and presentations, and while coaching to inspire, empower, motive and challenge people throughout the study of Human Excellence and Life Mastery Practices. Of course these amazing tools form the basis of all of my stress management programs, books and tools.

www.stressawarenessandprevention.com
www.thementalwellnessrevolution.com

Making Sense Of The Horrible Symptoms Of Stress, Anxiety, Panic Attacks, Burnout And Agoraphobia

As I have mentioned before, when suffering with debilitating stress we typically want, or need three things. We need to figure out what is really causing the stress in our lives, so that we can come up with a solution to resolve it. We need to quell the debilitating symptoms, so that we can feel more in control of our lives. And, we need to take a look at how we see ourselves with regards to stress, and how resourceful we think we are when it comes to handling life's challenges.

Although all three aspects are very important they do not necessarily need to be addressed in this order. However, when stress is interfering with how we live our life, and if it is affecting our health, wellness, relationships and overall happiness, we need to take immediate action. And under these circumstances, what most people want and need more than anything else, is to get rid of the horrible symptoms first.

Before we get started though I'm going to tell you a little about the therapies I used to quell my own symptoms. And I'll explain how and why they work.

The Truth About New Age, Holistic, Alternative, And Mind Body Therapies

If the idea of using new age, holistic, alternative and mind body therapies is new to you, and you are feeling a little skeptical, you are not alone. However, if you take a look around, you will notice how many integrative healing centers are popping up all around the world.

This trend is in part due to the fact that so many western trained doctors and therapists are becoming more aware of the benefits of alternative therapies, and the various healing arts.

This movement is also in part, a response to meet the demands of the ever growing population who want more choice in their lives. And there is nowhere that this is more evident, than where their health and wellbeing is concerned.

There truly is a health revolution underway. And thanks to the internet which has allowed us to take a glimpse at what is really going on in the world of health and wellness, millions of people are waking up, and noticing a shift in their own perception. This has brought about a new awareness of just how powerful many of these therapies can be. And we are also seeing how some are being, and have been used, as the primary source of healing for literally thousands of years. In fact various modalities of the healing arts have been practiced, and honored by many cultures throughout the entire world. And it seems as though this may have gone on since the beginning of time.

This awareness is igniting more interest, as well as fueling a movement amongst men and women from all walks of life who are actively seeking a more holistic, natural and hands on approach to their own, as well as their family's health and wellbeing.

As we all know, the right knowledge is power. It also gives us choice, and this is just one of the reasons why so many people are choosing to educate themselves on this subject. This awareness is allowing people to become far more proactive with their health, and in the process they're realizing just how important many of these therapies can be. Many are learning, and using these therapies for the benefits of personal wellness, as well as disease prevention and holistic healing for the body, mind and soul.

www.stressawarenessandprevention.com
www.thementalwellnessrevolution.com

Also, what this means is that, gone are the days when a life threatening diagnosis left a person with little choice other than to put their life in the hands of the medical establishments. And the very medical or mental health "professionals" whose reputations we daren't to have questioned.

Having the right knowledge gives us the power to question anything that doesn't feel right. It also gives us more choice. And it is this realization that is inspiring droves of people to empower themselves by doing their own research. In many cases people are also choosing to play a much more active role where their health and wellbeing is concerned.

The nice thing about this is that we no longer have to sit around just hoping and praying for the best, while feeling helpless. When we empower ourselves in such a way we tend to feel more hopeful and positive. These thoughts and emotions, along with the belief that we have the power to overcome so many of life's obstacles will likely contribute to strengthening our immune systems, and self healing powers.

One field of new age therapy which is of particular interest to me is that of energy, and the art of energy balancing. Not only does this often seem to work like magic, but it is one that absolutely anyone can learn, and practice on a daily basis. Energy balancing can also help a person maintain and enhance various aspects of their life, including their mental, emotional and physical health and wellbeing. In fact, it is probably the most important aspect of balancing a person's mind body system, and is the reason I encourage everyone to learn how to tap into their own mind body magic.

By learning how to tap into your own mind body magic you'll be joining the millions of people, from all around the world who are already using, or learning energy awareness and balancing. Not only do these exercises literally balance the mind body system, but in turn they can help a person become more connected, and improve communication with others. The process also improves mental clarity and focus, and allows an overall sense of wellbeing.

Energy balancing, and the other mind body modalities I work with, can also help to clear emotional trauma. As well as assist with healing physical health conditions, eliminate fears and phobias, and help a person break through life's challenges. These challenges may include issues such as clearing unconscious self sabotaging behaviours and limiting beliefs, as well as obstacles and objections. If left unchecked, many of these obstacles can, and often do prevent a person from experiencing success in any, or many areas of their life. However, by learning how to balance these self healing channels you may also notice improved confidence, and an overall sense of happiness and wellbeing These are just a few of the reasons why energy balancing and energy work are quickly becoming some of the fastest growing areas of personal interest in the world.

Tapping Into Your Mind Body Magic To Help Relieve The Symptoms Of Stress

Perhaps one of the most significant benefits of using mind body therapies to help combat the symptoms of stress, is that they acknowledge the fact that stress is a mind body experience. This is a very different belief to many of the western schools of thought, who often consider stress to be all in the head.

This is exactly why there has been so much emphasis put on "talk therapy". And although regular therapy can be useful for anyone who needs someone to talk to, it may not be that effective for quelling the horrible symptoms, of intense stress related conditions.

Doctors on the other hand, especially psychiatrists tend to focus more on the idea that the symptoms of stress are caused by a chemical imbalance. And with this belief comes the practice of attempting to correct these imbalances with chemicals, usually prescribed in the form of anti-anxiety medication, antidepressants, or some other type of psychotropic drugs. And although there are literally millions of people taking these medications on any given day, more and more are rejecting the idea while voicing their concerns about the side effects, and the safety of the drugs. These are likely some of the same people who are looking for a more natural and hands on approach to their health and wellbeing.

So What Do I Mean By Saying That Stress Is A Mind Body Experience

The fact that stress is a mind body experience should come as no surprise. Especially when you consider the fact that we humans, as well as all of the animals we share this planet with, are mind body entities. What this means is that every thought, whether positive or negative will elicit a certain set of feelings. If we think about a certain thing then it will elicit, or bring about certain feelings. And if we feel a certain way, if the feelings are strong enough, then they may generate associated thoughts.

To help you understand this concept a little better, just take a moment to think about something that causes you stress. This could be something you are worried about, such as a financial situation, a disagreement that you've had with someone, or a challenge you are facing in work. You could pick any situation where you want to experience change in your life, but you feel stuck, or even helpless. As you think about this experience, take a moment to scan your body and notice how, when you think about this negative situation, it makes you feel.

Often the things that we worry about will cause us to feel a whole slew of physical symptoms. These may include head, neck or backache, excess tiredness, upset stomach, shallow breathing, tensions throughout the body, or some strong emotions. As you can see it is very possible to experience these symptoms even though you may only be thinking about a problem, and not confronted by the issue in present time. This is because the thought is eliciting a mind body experience.

The reason that it is possible to feel these feelings when merely thinking about something is probably because everything that has ever happened to you, (including every experience you have ever had since the moment you were born, actually since the moment you were conceived) is stored in your mind body energy system. These experiences create what an individual now knows as their own personal "reality".

In other words, it is likely that any physical feelings or sensations which are generated during the time a person is exposed to a negative event, will become attached to the thoughts associated with that particular event. Together these thoughts and feelings make up an individual's personal experience, or reality. This will then be stored in the mind body system as a complete or whole experience. In the process theses experiences also create what we (especially those of us trained in and practicing NLP) call an anchor.

These anchors typically remain out of our awareness, or at least until they are triggered, or activated, at some point in time. When this happens, an anchor can have the power to bring back a memory. It could even bring forward into our present awareness a representation of what we believe to have been the original experience. Or what we now consider to be our own "reality".

www.stressawarenessandprevention.com
www.thementalwellnessrevolution.com

It is possible to trigger an anchor just by being exposed to anything that is associated to the original event, memory or perception. And this could be literally anything, which had been experienced by any of the senses. When triggered, an anchor will likely bring forward into your present awareness either a memory, visual pictures in your mind, recalled auditory experience (either something you had heard at the time, something you may imagine hearing under a similar situation, or perhaps even internal dialogue) or you could experience a kinesthetic mind body sensation. Alternatively, an anchor could also be triggered when one or more of the physical, or mind body elements which were present during the original experience, is present, or gets triggered within our mind body system.

The good news about this is that these anchors are also created around positive and happy experiences as well. And given the right tools they can also be dismantled, as in broken apart, to detach the negative feelings from a memory. This is one of the tools I use with my coaching clients to help them change the way they feel, or how they respond to specific situations that typically cause them discomfort. I demonstrate this tool in a program which I've developed specifically to help people overcome panic attacks.

www.stressawarenessandprevention.com
www.thementalwellnessrevolution.com

Following is an explanation of how an anchor can be created and locked into the mind body, or energy system.

Imagine that you are driving down the street and all of a sudden someone speeds through an intersection and smashes right into your car. Now besides any physical pain, any thoughts, feelings, fears or emotions which were activated, and present at the time of the accident, will all become melded together and will create an anchor.

The anchor will then be stored in your mind body energy system where it may be accessed, or triggered anytime you think about the accident, or are ever exposed to anything that reminds you of it. Since the whole experience has now been locked into the mind body system, it may even be triggered by any of the other variables (postural positions) which were present during this traumatic event. These may include: physical posture, such as the way you were sitting or the position of your head, the direction your eyes were looking, your energy levels or breathing patterns. They also include any thoughts or feelings that you experienced at the time of the event.

Triggering this anchor may cause you to re-experience some, or all of the physical, and/or emotional symptoms that were present at the time of the original experience. Which, in this case I am referring to the accident.

In other words, there doesn't necessarily have to be a thought or a memory of the original event present in order to have the mind body experience triggered again. In fact, the trigger could instead be any of the physical aspects, such as a feeling or any of the postural position that were present during or around the time of the original event. So, as you can see, it could just as likely be a physical movement or a body sensation that would trigger the mind body experience. And in turn it would illicit, or bring back some or all of the memories, thoughts, or feelings that had been present, or generated during that original event.

What this means is that these anchors may then be triggered anytime you drive through the same intersection, or are exposed to a similar experience. This could include: driving through any intersection, driving in specific situations, driving in certain weather conditions, travelling as a passenger, or even the thought of having to drive. If an anchor is strong enough it could bring the original mind body experience back into present time, and possibly even create a phobia. This is when we may see someone who becomes terrified of driving in general, driving in certain specific situations, getting into a car as a passenger, or possibly even using any form of transportation.

Anchors can be extremely powerful, and even though we may not actually be consciously aware of them, they can be created, and may positively or negatively affect absolutely any area of a person's life. And while positive anchors may bring us a great deal of pleasure. A person who has multiple negative anchors may become so stressed and overwhelmed, that they could end up feeling as though life is just too much to handle. This is why I put a great deal of emphasis on teaching people how to become aware of their own personal anchors. I also teach them how to dismantle the ones that they no longer want, and to build more positive and empowering new anchors instead.

Let's now take a look at what happens on a mind body level when a person becomes stressed, or when one of these very negative anchors is triggered.

Stress, And The Mind Body Reaction

When stressed, blood rushes from our frontal brain lobes, where we do much of our creative thinking and decision making, to the back of the brain where it plays an important role in activating the survival mechanism. This is also known as the fight or flight response. When this happens we usually feel overwhelmed and confused, and may have difficulty thinking clearly. In turn we are more likely to react poorly to problems or perceived threats, instead of being able to come up with creative or rational solutions. Ever wonder why you can't think straight when stressed?

Then there is the issue of the electromagnetic energy system which flows thorough, and around every living thing. This includes humans, animals and plants. And even though some scholars within the world of western medicine have now acknowledged it's existence, some still have trouble accepting this fact. Regardless, this energy flows continuously throughout our entire lives and primarily runs through our meridian system. There are two main meridians called The Central Meridian and The Governing meridian that supports all of the other meridians. Each one is associated with an organ, a muscle group and an emotion. This is probably why our energy is affected by our thoughts and feelings, or our mental or emotional states.

When all is well this energy flows freely and helps to keep our physical, mental and emotional health in balance. However, when stressed the energy can become disrupted or blocked, and this sets off a whole sequence of negative effects. Here is a simplistic explanation of how stress and/or a fear can affect our energy system.

First imagine water running through a hose pipe. Then imagine that the hose gets a kink in it which in turn disrupts the flow of the water, and prevents it from running freely through the hose.

The stress or fear response works in very much the same way. As I have already mentioned, we all have life energy flowing through our bodies on a continuous basis. Much like when water runs through a hosepipe. When we encounter something that puts stress on this system, whether it is a fear, a negative emotional experience, an allergen, or an energy toxin, we may experience what is known as an energy disruption, or a block in the energy flow. Such a disruption could have a similar effect on the body's energy flow, as what a kink in a hosepipe would have on the water that had been running through it. When you experience such a disruption your energy can no longer flow freely, and your energy force may plummet. This can easily be demonstrated with muscle testing.

Depending on the intensity of the fear or stress in the mind body system, will determine how aware you will be of any negative effect it could be having on your body. Your physical energy may drop, causing you to suddenly feel weak. I have been told that our energy can plummet by about 80%, and this is why it is advisable to have a person sit down if you ever need to deliver some bad news. This energy disruption can also affect the brain by causing the brain hemispheres to have difficulty communicating with each other (ever wonder why you can't think straight while in a stressful situation?). And the fight or flight response may kick in, meaning that you will experience a whole slew of scary sensations as the body responds to what it now perceives as a threat.

I just want to say that although the fight or flight response can be one of the most terrifying experiences to have to live through, it is a wonderful example of just how intelligent the mind body system is. And it has been because of my own experience with panic attacks that I became aware of this. And through my realization of how brilliant this system is I have now became fascinated with fear. In turn I have developed some powerful programs to help people combat different types of fears. I call this my strange fascination with fear.

So you are probably wondering why this is so relevant and how it all fits into everyday stress. Well you see, not only do these anchors literally play a huge role in how we experience everyday life by eliciting thoughts and feelings from past experiences. But, we are also capable of experiencing the same feelings and sensations even when we are merely thinking about things that may not have even happened yet. Or for that matter, they may never actually happen at all. This may be in part due to the fact that, as brilliant as our brains are, they don't seem to be able to differentiate between what is real and what is imagined. Therefore the brain can trigger a mind body experience just by thinking about something, and then tricking the body into believing it is real.

What this means is that it could be very possible to illicit the exact same emotional response, and sometimes even similar physical feelings and sensations for something that we are merely thinking about, or imagining, as it is, for an event that has actually happened in the past. And if this is so, then it could also be possible for a person to spend a great deal of their life stressed out, and therefore experiencing all of the uncomfortable physical symptoms of stress, simply by thinking about, or anticipating something that may never actually happen at all.

www.stressawarenessandprevention.com
www.thementalwellnessrevolution.com

This is what happens when a person worries about something that may or may not even happen in the future. Now this is not to say that their worries are not warranted. But wouldn't it be useful, and more advantageous to be able to put these negative symptoms and feelings of overwhelm on hold? At least until we know for sure whether or not we do have something to actually be concerned about? After all, if we could master this skill it would allow us to be able to think more clearly and rationally, and in turn come up with some creative solutions to our problems.

Instead, most people literally become consumed by their worries, and this in itself could be detrimental to their health. They then start to notice the physical and sometimes weird sensations throughout their bodies, as well as the emotional stress. These symptoms which were probably caused by the stress in the first place often result in a person wondering if they could be seriously ill. This then causes them to become even more worried and concerned about their physical health, causing the cycle of stress to spiral deeper out of control.

This is how easy it can be for everyday stress to spiral out of control and manifest into anxiety, panic attacks, burnout and agoraphobia. By now the victim of what started out as stress may become so overwhelmed that they may not even recognize what caused the stress in the first place. Nor will he/she realize that the stress contributed to the state they may now be in, which by now may even have become incapacitating.

Sadly this is where so many people then turn to drugs or alcohol, or they participate in other addictive behaviours in order to try to mask their symptoms. This can be the beginning of a lifelong problem of addiction, possibly even becoming addicted to pharmaceutical medications.

These thoughts and the associated feelings also put us into what is known as a state. A state is a mind body experience which encompasses our thoughts, feelings, posture, breathing patterns and eye movements. A state may be positive or it may be negative, and whether we realize it or not we spend our entire lives shifting in and out of these different states. However we are typically only aware of the really high states, or the really low ones. With stress being a very good example of an intense state and depression an excellent example of a very low one. Hence the saying, she's gotten herself into a right state!

www.stressawarenessandprevention.com
www.thementalwellnessrevolution.com

I'm sure by now that you can see how stress is in fact a mind body experience, and how easy it can be for it to spiral out of control. But more importantly I hope that you now see the value of incorporating mind body therapies into your daily life. As they could possibly help you keep your mind body system in balance.

It was only after I had realized this for myself, that I reached a turning point and embraced the idea of learning about, and putting these New Age and Mind Body Therapies to the test. And thankfully, it was this decision, and the experiences that followed that allowed me to finally start getting well.

Many of the exercises I write about, and teach, are very easy to use, self help, mind body tools that allow a person to tap into their own mind body energy, and healing system. These exercises help to correct the energy flow in the meridians, as well as to rebalance the energy in the brain hemispheres allowing you to feel more balanced, centered, connected, grounded, calm and relaxed.

www.stressawarenessandprevention.com
www.thementalwellnessrevolution.com

The Stress Less Approach To Conquering Your Stress, Anxiety, Panic Attacks, Burnout And Agoraphobia

I always say that whenever we find ourselves suffering with any of these debilitating conditions that we need to address three things. We need to find a way to quell the symptoms. We need to identify the causes. And, we need to take a look at how we see ourselves in relation to how stress affects us, in other words, how the stress in our lives can taint our identity. And since one of the first things that we need, or perhaps want most of all is to be able to quell the horrible symptoms, I'm going to address this one first.

However, before we jump into the exercises that help alleviate the symptoms, I want to introduce you to some very common, yet seldom recognized roadblocks. The roadblocks, which are so often overlooked, can and often do prevent healing in any area of a person's life.

However, the sad truth is, that the reason they are so often ignored, is because most people, including many "professionals" are not even aware that they exist. Yet, unless they are addressed, you may find it very difficult to experience any positive or long lasting change. This is especially so for anyone who suffers with such debilitating conditions as anxiety, panic attacks, agoraphobia, fears or addictions.

Roadblocks To Successful Healing

One of the most fascinating discoveries of energy balancing is the realization that there are some imbalances which can literally sabotage or hinder any healing process. These saboteurs can affect anyone and are commonly known as Psychological Reversal (PR), Neurological Disorganization (ND), Switching, and Individual Energy Toxins (IET). These conditions are known to cause confusion, or what may seem like a form of unconscious self sabotage. However, with the appropriate mind body exercises and remedies they can quite easily be corrected.

Following is a description of some of the roadblocks which you may encounter, as well as an explanation of some of the exercises which may be used to correct them. It is often necessary to do the following exercises before moving on and attempting any of the others.

Psychological Reversal (PR)

Psychological Reversal is the name coined by Dr. Roger Callahan for the phenomenon which seems to prevent people from achieving certain things in their life. This phenomenon which is apparently caused by what is known as an energy, or polarity reversal, is also often seen as a block to healing in the mental, emotional, or physical body. It is almost like an unconscious, self sabotaging force, and can prevent even the most motivated person from experiencing success in any or all areas of their life. It is typical to see this reversal in people who suffer with any type of fear, phobia, stress or addictive behaviour which they just can't seem to overcome.

The correction for PR is to rebalance the energy block or reversal, which may otherwise prevent any actual correction from being successful. Since this is not the actual algorithm for the problem itself, a TFT practitioner would first check for PR. Then, if necessary correct it before having a client perform the tapping sequence which has been selected for the specific issue. This sequence would most likely be unique to an individual, especially if it were identified with the help of muscle checking. A process which overrides an individual's preprogrammed analytical beliefs and instead gathers information directly from a person's mind body system.

Mind Body Exercise For Correcting Psychological Reversal (PR)

The correction point for PR is called the Karate Chop Point, or KC, as it is located on the side of the hand about 1 inch up from the base of the little finger. It is the part of the hand that you would use if you were going to give someone a karate chop, although what we are actually doing is stimulating the meridian.

To perform this treatment, simply use your index finger and the one next to it to tap the KC point on the other hand. Give it 5-15 good solid taps before switching hands, and repeating on the other hand. There are also variations of this exercise that can be used in different situations. One of which I demonstrate in my Stress Less Driving App, suggesting that you literally karate chop the steering wheel while sitting at a traffic light. Or when feeling stressed out when stuck in a traffic jam.

KC Tapping Point is located on the outside edge of hand.

Tap KC Point with 2 fingers of other hand. about 15-30 tap

When Should You Do This Exercise

You should do the PR exercise prior to doing any TFT correction. You can also do it anytime you are having negative thoughts, or if you are feeling stressed, anxious or confused.

Neurological Disorganization (ND)

The exercise to correct neurological disorganization is called The Collarbone Breathing Exercise. Dr. Roger Callahan recommends that you do this during the TFT treatment, if the treatment seems to have stalled. Meaning that, you've reached a point where the intensity of the stress or fear will not drop any lower. However, I personally love this exercise and have found it to be so powerful that I've used it whenever I've felt overwhelmed or been faced with a very stressful situation.

For example, one day I had to go to a meeting which I knew was going to be highly confrontational. It was with a woman who I worked with and I was not in a position to defend myself against. I prepared for the meeting by doing the ND exercise, while I thought about how I was expecting the meeting to go.

On my way to the meeting I felt really nervous with anticipation. However, as soon as I arrived and was confronted by this woman's verbally abusive attack, the strangest thing happened. As I stood there I became very aware of how her outburst wasn't having any impact on me at all. In fact, since my response to her behaviour was obviously not what she expected, she became even more irate. Her face was turning red, the veins were almost bursting out of her neck, and she was literally shaking, and yet I didn't feel at all intimidated or nervous. In fact, because my calm state enabled me to just stand there and watch her losing control, the whole incident turned out to be an extremely empowering experience for me.

Looking back I now realize that I should have done this exercise while thinking about driving to the meeting as well. As I'm sure that if I had done so I would have felt much less anxious about that part too.

To perform the Collarbone Breathing exercise, simply follow the steps below. There are two parts of this exercise. One part is a sequence of tapping on meridian points to help balance the meridians, while the other part is a breathing sequence.

Tapping Sequence

There are two meridian points to pay attention to for this exercise. The first being what Dr. Roger Callahan (TFT) refers to as the collarbone tapping points. These are actually the K27 Kidney meridian points, and the other is often called the gamut point.

The K27 or collarbone point can be located by placing your index fingers at the base of the throat where a person would knot a tie. Then slide the fingers down about 1 inch and then approximately 1 inch to either side. You will find an indentation at each point. The K27 points are actually the last points of the Kidney Meridians.

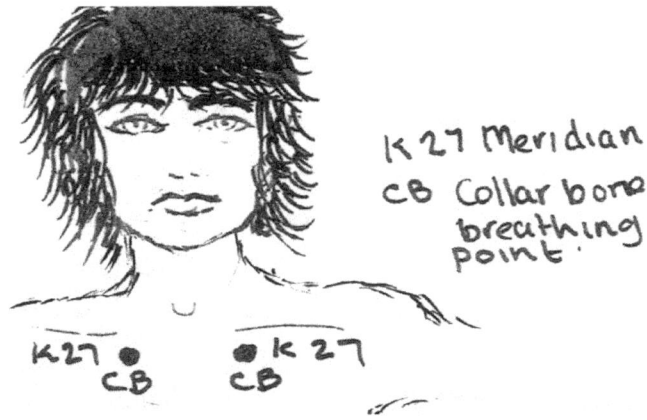

The Gamut Point can be found on the back of the hand about ½ -1 inch up from the base of the ring finger and baby finger or the 3rd and 4th fingers. This is the Tipple Heater meridian.

To perform this tapping sequence, simply take the tips of your index and middle finger of one hand, and place them on either one of the collarbone points (K27). Then, using the tips of your index and middle figure of the other hand, tap on the Gamut Point (on the back of the hand) of the hand which is touching the K27

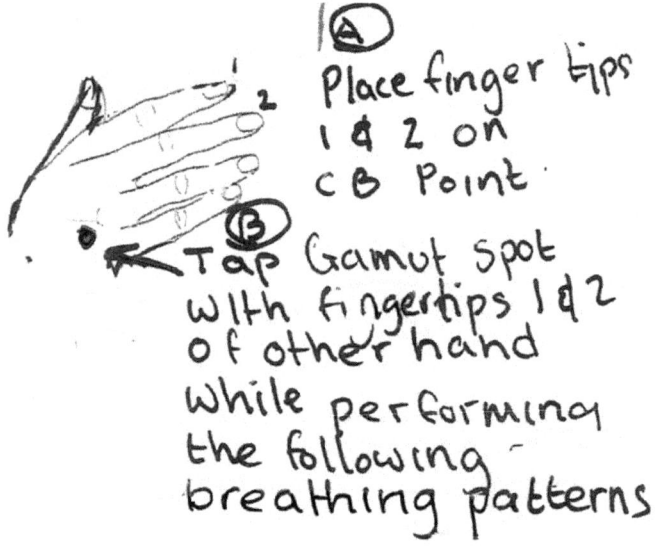

Ⓐ Place finger tips 1 & 2 on CB Point.
Ⓑ Tap Gamut spot with fingertips 1 & 2 of other hand while performing the following breathing patterns

While you are doing this you will perform the 5 breathing sequences listed below. Then repeat the exact same exercise with the same 2 fingers placed on the other collarbone point. When you have finished that, switch hands and repeat exactly the same sequence with the other hand.

Breathing Patterns

Take a deep breath in and hold for a few seconds

Let half of the breath out and hold

Let all of the breath out and hold

Take half a breath in and hold

Breathe normally

Next you are going to repeat the entire exercise again. Only this time instead of placing your finger tips on the collarbone point, you are going to use your knuckles. To achieve this simply bend your index and middle finger, and place the knuckles of those two fingers on the K27 or collarbone points. Keep your elbows raised up to the sides (not tucked into your body) and keep your thumbs up and away from your body. From this position, you will then perform the same tapping sequence (using the tips of the fingers of the other hand) on the gamut spot. Don't forget to repeat the breathing exercises.

www.stressawarenessandprevention.com
www.thementalwellnessrevolution.com

You will find a video of these tapping exercises on my website www.suzanneprice.com

When Should You Do This Exercise

You can do this exercise anytime you are feeling confused, overwhelmed, stressed or anxious. I also like to do it if my mind is filled with negative thoughts, or while I'm thinking through any event which I anticipate being stressful. I definitely recommend doing it prior to doing any TFT exercise.

Dealing With Past Negative Experiences

When we've suffered a traumatic experience which has become locked into our mind body system as an anchor, the whole experience could potentially be triggered again. This could happen anytime we find ourselves exposed to something that reminds us of the original event, and can cause all of the memories and their associated feelings to come flooding back to haunt us.

When this happens not only will this remind us of just how uncomfortable the original experience was, but it may also serve as evidence, that this anchor could potentially be triggered again. This in itself could have the power to prevent a person, or at least deter them from taking similar risks in the future, and could even create an avoidance pattern.

Some people put so much attention on their past experiences that they may find it almost impossible to even imagine being able to change how they feel. And many will even use these past negative experiences to defend being stuck in their lives, and they will continue to do so no matter how uncomfortable their life may be. They may feel as though they are stuck in a certain area of their life and they have the evidence to prove why things are so bad for them. And some will even unwittingly use their past negative experience as a reason not to move forward. Others will desperately want to change their lives and will try anything in their power to do so. Yet it may seem as though the thoughts, and feelings, which had become attached to these past events keep popping up, and preventing them from ever moving on.

This is often the case for anyone who has suffered with an extremely intense panic attack. And it is at times like this, that it would be helpful if we could literally detach any negative feelings from the memories which became melded together during the original traumatic experience. By doing so we may be able to avert another attack.

www.stressawarenessandprevention.com
www.thementalwellnessrevolution.com

Following are a few exercises that I found to be very powerful for helping me do just that, detaching the thoughts from the feelings. This process helped me dismantle the anchors that were causing a lot of my ongoing stress.

TFT Algorithm For Trauma

Since I have suffered with panic attacks I know how traumatic they can be. Therefore I would recommend that you use the Trauma TFT Algorithm to help neutralize the feelings associated with any past attacks. Also, since most people feel shame or embarrassment as a result of not feeling in control of their lives. Or they are afraid of embarrassing themselves by having a panic attack in front of others, I have added in a couple of additional tapping points. They help deal with the dreaded shame, and fear of embarrassment which often accompany this condition.

If you suffer with panic attacks on a regular basis and are looking to put an end to them, then you might want to check out my program. It is called Take Control Of Panic Attacks, The Same Way I Did. I designed this program specifically to help people overcome panic attacks, and include many of the tools which I personally used to put an end

www.stressawarenessandprevention.com
www.thementalwellnessrevolution.com

to my own anxiety, panic attacks, burnout and agoraphobia.

Past Trauma Algorithm With Anger, Guilt & Embarrassment

Do the following exercise while thinking of a panic attack which you have had in the past.

For TFT to be effective you must be tuned into the problem. This means that at the very least, you need to be thinking about the problem which caused the attack, or of the attack itself. If you are not sure what caused it, then simply perform the exercises while thinking of something that you feel could be relevant to why you suffered the attack. Then while keeping this thought in mind, perform the following algorithm.

*See diagram on following page which shows tapping points

Eb, E, A, C, TF, C, IF, C, UN

Using the tips of your fingers, tap on the following tapping points while thinking of the problem (in this case the problem would be the previous panic attack).

www.stressawarenessandprevention.com
www.thementalwellnessrevolution.com

Eb	Beginning of eyebrow (closest to center of face/nose)
E	Under eye (just below the pupil on bone)
A	Under arm – in line with the nipples of a man
C	Collarbone – K27 (same as point in Collarbone Breathing Exercise)
TF	Tiny Finger (little finger on side of nail bed)
C	Collarbone – K27 (same as point in Collarbone Breathing Exercise)
IF	Index Finger Nail (on the side of nail bed closest to the thumb)
C	Collarbone – K27 (same as point in Collarbone Breathing Exercise)
UN	Underneath the nose (center between the tip of nose and upper lip)

www.stressawarenessandprevention.com
www.thementalwellnessrevolution.com

Diagram Of Tapping Point

Relieve Stress, Anxiety, Burnout, Panic Attacks & Agoraphobia
The Same Way I Did

Part 2

While still thinking of the problem - tap the Gamut or brain balancer spot on the back of the hand. You will find this about ½" to 1" up from the base of the fingers, between the ring finger and the little finger. Tap continuously while performing the following sequence. See diagram below.

Eyes open

Eyes closed

Eyes down right

Eyes down left

Big circle right

Big circle left

Hum a tune

Count to 10 – then count backwards

Hum a tune

www.stressawarenessandprevention.com
www.thementalwellnessrevolution.com

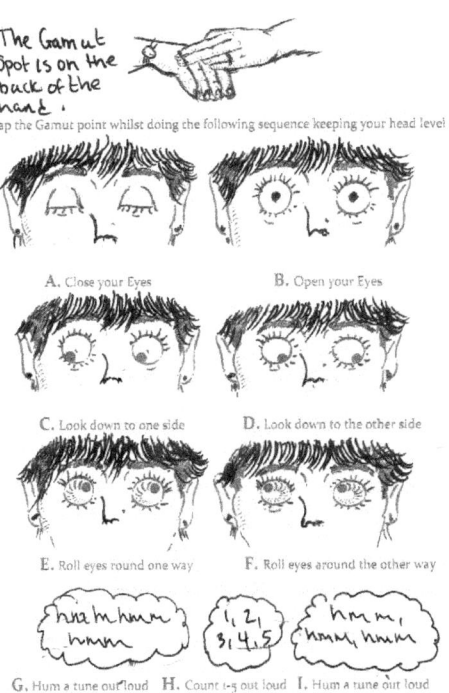

Relieve Stress, Anxiety, Burnout, Panic Attacks & Agoraphobia
The Same Way I Did

www.stressawarenessandprevention.com
www.thementalwellnessrevolution.com

Part 3

Repeat First Sequence Eb, E, A, C, TF, C, IF, C, UN

Eb	Beginning of eyebrow (closest to center of face/nose)
E	Under eye (just below the pupil)
A	Under arm – in line with the nipples of a man
C	Collarbone – K27 (same as point in Collarbone Breathing Exercise)
TF	Tiny (little) Finger
C	Collarbone – K27 (same as point in Collarbone Breathing Exercise)
IF	Index Finger Nail (on the side closest to the thumb)
C	Collarbone – K27 (same as point in Collarbone Breathing Exercise)
UN	Underneath the nose (center between the tip of nose and upper lip)

www.stressawarenessandprevention.com
www.thementalwellnessrevolution.com

When Should You Do This Exercise?

You could do this exercise while thinking of any past negative experience that still plays a role in sabotaging any, present or future events. This past experience could have been a panic attack. Or it could have been any other negative experience which has happened in the past, but still influences how you react to certain things, events, or situations in present time. This includes any memories that cause you to avoid certain situations that would otherwise be neutral, or positive, if it weren't for the negative anchor of the old experience.

NLP Putting Your Past Negative Experience Behind You

After completing the algorithm for a past trauma, I'm going to suggest that you lock it into place with this NLP exercise. To do so, you will need to imagine yourself sitting in a movie theatre. Up on the screen in front of you, you will notice a still photo of the negative event or experience which took place. Take a look at the screen to see if you can see yourself up there in the photo, as if someone else, perhaps a bystander had taken a photo of the scene with you in it (this is what we call disassociated). Or, are you seeing an image of the scene, as you saw it through your own eyes, at the time of the stressful event. (This is what we call associated)

If necessary change that picture so that you can see yourself up there on the screen, as if someone had taken a photo of the event and you are now seeing what a bystander would have seen. Then, in your mind, see the screen shrink down to a smaller size. You can make it as small as you like. Notice how you feel as the picture gets smaller.

Then, imagine taking hold of the two top corners, folding them in towards each other, and then scrunching the whole thing up into a ball. Notice that the screen is actually made of a very fragile type of tissue paper which is breaking apart and disintegrating as you handle it. Scrunch it up into a little ball making it as small as you can. When you are ready, throw that ball of paper up into the air, and up over your head behind you. Throw it as hard as you can, letting it take off into space where it will pick up speed. Take comfort in knowing that, as this ball of paper moves further and further away from you, it will break up and burn out, much like a comet would.

If you have difficulty with this exercise and find that you can't visualize the ball of energy taking off, or if it seems that the memory keeps popping up in your mind, just go through the exercise again. Don't worry about it too much. Just trust the process, knowing that you have started to put that past negative experience (an event that has already taken place therefore it is in your past) behind you. This is where it now belongs, once and for all.

When Should You Do This Exercise

You should do this exercise to finish off any process that you have been working on to clear past negative events. Or whenever a past negative event pops up in your mind and bothers you.

Moving Forward

How To Diffuse Potentially Stressful Future Events

Now that you have started to chip away at, or dismantle some of the past negative experiences which have acted as negative anchors. It is time to start focussing on changing the way you experience future events. The goals should be to limit stress and anxiety by breaking apart any anchors which could otherwise bring back negative emotions or feelings. To create some additional powerful resources which you could implement whenever you needed them, and to have more empowering, and pleasurable experiences throughout your life.

In order to do this I am going to suggest that you do the following exercises. They are similar to the ones which helped me overcome my own anxiety, panic attacks, burnout and agoraphobia. And they are made up of a combination of TFT, NLP, One Brain Learning Awareness and TFH.

TFT Stress

Tap on the following tapping points whenever you feel stressed, anxious or panicky. Or while thinking of a future event which would normally make you feel anxious, or which has caused you to have a panic attack in the past.

EB, E, A, C

- Eb   Beginning of eyebrow (center of face closest to nose)
- E   Under eye (just below the pupil on bone)
- A   Under arm – in line with the nipples of a man
- C   Collarbone – K27 (same as point in Collarbone Breathing Exercise)

www.stressawarenessandprevention.com
www.thementalwellnessrevolution.com

While still thinking of the problem - tap the Gamut or brain balancer on the back of the hand, about ½" to 1" up from the base of the fingers, between the ring finger and the little finger. Tap continuously while performing the following sequence.

Eyes open

Eyes closed

Eyes down right

Eyes down left

Big circle right

Big circle left

Hum a tune

Count to 10 – then count backwards

Hum a tune

Repeat First Sequence

Eb   Beginning of eyebrow (center)

E   Under eye (just below the pupil)

A   Under arm – in line with the nipples of a man

C   Collarbone – K27 (same as point in Collarbone Breathing Exercise)

Tips & Tools From My Stress Less Boot Camp

When stressed blood rushes from our frontal brain lobes where we do much of our creative thinking and decision making, to the back of the brain where it plays an important role in activating the survival mechanism. This is also known as the fight or flight response. When this happens we usually feel overwhelmed and confused, and may have difficulty thinking clearly. Then instead of being able to come up with possible solutions to a problem, or make smart decisions, we may be more likely to react poorly, based on past experiences of similar stressful events.

This knee jerk reaction is a very useful response to have whenever we find ourselves faced with danger. This would mean that our survival instincts have kicked in, and could potentially save our life. Stopping to think about our options in such dire circumstances could cause us to react too slowly. Such a delay could result in us getting seriously hurt, or even killed in the process.

However, if on the other hand we overreact to every day stressors we may find ourselves living in a state of hyper vigilance, or even a heightened state of anxiety. This could ultimately play havoc on our health.

When we find ourselves in these stressful situations, and having difficulty trying to think rationally, we need to bring ourselves back into balance. Here are a few of my favourite tools that will help you become more centered and focused again.

Future Pace While Holding Neurovascular Holding Points

As I mentioned earlier, the fight or flight response causes us to react quickly, as opposed to allowing our brain to take its sweet time. This response increases our likelihood of survival in a life threatening situation. However, in order for this to happen, it appears as though our creative thinking center (in the front of the brain) becomes temporarily disabled and is likely the reason why, we have such great difficulty thinking rationally when stressed.

The following exercise is believed to counteract this particular reaction to stress, by helping to restore the energy flow back to the forebrain.

www.stressawarenessandprevention.com
www.thementalwellnessrevolution.com

How To Do This Exercise

Using the finger tips of both hands, apply a very light pressure, or touch to the Neurovascular points on the forehead. They are located above the eyebrows, about halfway between the brow and natural hair line, and between the midline of the face and the pupils. These are the frontal eminences. This is believed to have a soothing effect on the meridian energy of the forebrain, the area where the higher order thinking center is located. This part of the brain allows us to be creative, generate ideas, and come up with solutions to problems.

You can hold these points yourself, or have someone else hold them for you while you think through a particular problem. This is also a very effective tool to help you work through a past negative experience, or some sort of future event that you anticipate being negative.

The interesting thing is that we often unconsciously activate these points whenever we find ourselves in certain situations. For instance, it is not uncommon for a person to automatically place their hand on their forehead when trying to recall something. Such as, when we are trying to remember a name, or recall a memory. And we do

www.stressawarenessandprevention.com
www.thementalwellnessrevolution.com

this even though we are not even aware of the fact that we are doing it, never mind why.

Trace Your Brain Balancing Meridian

When stressed we often experience a disruption of energy in our meridian system. This will likely cause the energy to become reversed or blocked, or over or under energized. Most of the meridians are associated with a specific organ, a muscle group, and an emotion. This is why an imbalanced meridian will likely lead to an imbalance in our emotional state. In order to correct this state we need to rebalance the energy in the appropriate meridian.

The two main meridians, which are called the Central and Governing Meridians, affect the rest of the system. The central meridian runs up the front of the body, from the pubic bone to just below the bottom lip. This is the meridian which affects the energy to the brain. The governing meridian runs up the back of the body where it starts at the tailbone, runs up and over the top of the head, and ends just above the upper lip. The two connect inside the mouth, just behind the top front teeth, right in the center.

As long as we keep these two meridians balanced they will positively affect the entire meridian system. In order to ensure that the right amount of energy is flowing to the brain we need to correct the imbalance of the central meridian. Normally this imbalance would be detected by a practitioner who would use muscle testing to determine which meridian is in need of rebalancing. However, if you know that you are stressed or are experiencing difficulty thinking clearly then by all means go ahead and rebalance your own meridians. It is also good to do this if you are experiencing poor concentration, or feeling confused or overwhelmed.

The good news is that it is quite easy to rebalance the central meridian, and you can do it as often as you like. I like to start by doing a meridian flush. For this exercise you can use either the palm of your hand, or if you prefer, just one or two of your fingers. Holding your hand approximately 3 inches away from your body and starting at the pubic bone trace the central meridian up the entire length of the torso to just below the lower lip. Then sweep the energy back down to the starting position. Repeat this motion 3 times, being sure to end the circuit at the lip. On completion you can actually end by pressing gently on the spot just below the bottom lip, in the centre. It is that simple.

You don't always have to do the meridian flush. In fact if you were sitting in class and noticed yourself feeling tired or zoned out, you can trace the meridian from the pubic bone to the bottom lip. End the trace by placing your finger on that centre point just below the bottom lip. If on the other hand you are feeling over energized, or strung out, do the trace in reverse by tracing your meridian in a downward position. Then place the tip of your tongue just behind the top front teeth. This connects the central and governing meridians and helps to rebalance the brain hemispheres.

Either of these exercises will help to rebalance the normal flow of energy, and should clear any energy blocks which may have been caused by stress. Just remember though that it is important to finish at the top of the meridian trace if you want to re-energize, and at the bottom if you need to lower the energy.

Drink Water

Believe it or not dehydration can be a major source of stress. Knowing this, then it should go without saying that rehydration is the perfect remedy for this particular problem. In saying that, it is important that we consume pure drinking water for this purpose, and to help support the body.

Our bodies need water for every one of its systems to function properly. The lymphatic system needs water to carry waste and toxins away that could otherwise build up, putting stress on our bodily functions, and allowing disease to manifest. Our nervous system also needs water for the electrical impulses which carry orders from the brain to the muscles, and then feedback back to the brain, to function properly. Every organ needs water to function at its best, as does every single cell in the body. We need water for proper coordination, and unless we are getting enough our bodies will become stressed.

Some of the symptoms of dehydration include: feeling tired, overheated, irritable, thirsty or hungry. It can cause a person to feel light headed, it can cause headaches and muscles tension, and in extreme cases may even cause a person to pass out.

The good news is that dehydration can easily be remedied by drinking water. This will increase mental and physical energy, improve clarity of thinking, reduce stress on the heart and lungs, and assist with coordination. When we drink pure water it is recognized by receptors in the mouth which then send a message to the brain letting it know that all is well, and this can instantly correct the stress response.

www.stressawarenessandprevention.com
www.thementalwellnessrevolution.com

Although some will tell you that it doesn't matter what you drink as long as you are taking in fluids, other's claim that we do need to drink pure water in order to reap the benefits.

Cross Patterning

The following exercise which is known as cross patterning or cross crawling is so easy to do. Yet it can help quell the symptoms of stress. It works by stimulating the integration between the brain hemispheres. This is so important because the left and right brain hemispheres control approximately 80% of the motor neurons of the muscles, in the opposite side of the body.

This exercise also moves lymph through the lymphatic system, clearing stress producing toxins from the body. It also helps to improve concentration, coordination and focus, increases energy levels, and may also have a positive impact on dyslexia.

To do this exercise properly, simply start by marching on the spot. Raise one arm (extended out in front of you), while raising the opposite leg (as if you were going to take a big step up), at the same time. Exaggerate the movement by crossing the arm over the midline of the body, as if you were adding a slight twist, or going to touch the opposite knee. Do exactly the same movement on the other side. Repeat until you have completed about 30-50 knee raises on each side. This exercise will help to fire off both brain hemispheres.

Next, switch the marching style so that you raise both the arm, and the knee of the same side of the body, at the same time. This should feel a little awkward. Repeat on the other side and continue until you have done about 30 – 50 reps on each side.

Finally, go back and repeat the first pattern. Touch opposite hand to knee, repeat until you have completed 30-50 reps on each side.

Continue to switch back and forth between the 2 marching styles until you have completed at least 7 sets of each movement, or until you become completely comfortable with the exercise. Make sure that you finish up with the last set being the one where you are touching the opposite leg to hand. This exercise can be adapted by touching your toe or heel to the ground in front of you, or kicking your heel up behind you to touch the opposite hand. To make it a little more fun, try doing this to music.

Rescue Remedy

After trying many different natural therapies I found my favourites, with one of them being Rescue Remedy. This concoction of flower essences makes up what I believe to be one of nature's little miracle helpers. And the reason that I love it so much, is that it is one of the few things that I've ever tried that offered me almost instant relief.

When I say that it offers relief, it does not necessarily stop a panic attack in its tracks, but then again I don't believe anything can. However, what it does seem to do is offer a calming effect in a very short amount of time.

I also love the fact that it is natural, and considered to be safe enough to be given to children and pets. As with anything else though you should check with your doctor before taking this or any other natural products, and be sure to talk to a wellness advisor about how best to take it.

Rescue remedy is available in several forms, including drops, topical cream, spray, or pastilles, all offer amazing results. When suffering with my debilitating stress and anxiety I used the drops. I had not tried the pastilles until I recently won a tin at a presentation on Bach Flowers. I'd forgotten that I had them until one day I was put on the spot and asked to do a presentation which was to take place in a matter of hours. I agreed to do it, but since I had no time to prepare, nor did I really know what I was going to talk about I felt a little stressed. In fact as I sat waiting to be introduced to the group I felt pangs of nervousness in my stomach, and shooting through my body.

While reaching into my purse to get a tic-tac I saw the Rescue Remedy pastilles, so I decided to try one. No sooner had I put the pastille in my mouth and my nervousness completely disappeared, leaving me in a state of calm. I remained in this positive and calm state for the rest of the time I was waiting as well as throughout my entire presentation.

Rescue remedy is a combination of 5 of the flower remedies created by Dr. Edward Bach, a British surgeon and bacteriologist who turned to homeopathy and joined the Royal London Homeopathic Hospital. Dr. Bach eventually developed these remedies from the flower essences which proved to have the power to correct emotional imbalances. This was accomplished by replacing a negative emotion with a corresponding positive one instead. Bach Remedies claim that their remedies are safe to use on animals as well as children. I have personally used them on animals and have seen great results with kids.

To administer the Rescue Remedy you simply put a few drops under your tongue, or drop them into your drinking water. When using them on animals simply put the remedy onto your fingers so that you can then gently massage them into your pet's ears. Do NOT put the drops into your pet's mouth as they are suspended in alcohol, and this can make the animal feel ill. There is now a Rescue Remedy formula which has been developed specifically for animals; however I have not used this particular product.

Rescue remedy has also been found very useful for helping people who suffer with a condition called psychological reversal. This is the phenomenon I wrote about in the section on roadblocks to recovery, as it is usually present in anyone who is stressed or anxious. PR can cause confusion in the brain body system and is sometimes seen as a form of unconscious self sabotage. It can apparently hinder healing of any kind. Including, preventing a person from overcoming an emotional problem, or it can cause someone to become stuck in life, or behave in self sabotaging ways. PR can even be a block to personal success.

One of the most obvious cases I've seen of PR was a woman who was chronically reversed following a traumatic event. In fact, it was almost impossible to help her even with TFT because she kept slipping back into a Reversed State. Even when we would correct the reversal she would switch back, preventing her from completing the TFT sequence. While in a training in Seattle she took some of the Rescue Remedy Pastilles, which helped her to complete the TFT sequence, which consequently benefited her greatly.

I personally feel that Bach Remedies are a great supplement to mind body and energy balancing techniques.

www.stressawarenessandprevention.com
www.thementalwellnessrevolution.com

Learn To Identify Exactly Where Your Stress Is Coming From

In order to be able to truly manage your stress you must first become clear about what is causing it. This awareness will allow you to make some different choices and possibly even come up with some solutions. However one of the challenges of suffering with stress is that it can become so overwhelming. And when this happens the only things we may then be aware of are the uncomfortable symptoms or the problems which have arisen as a result of becoming stressed.

Ironically this overwhelm may inhibit us from even recognizing the cause of our own stress, meaning that it would remain out of our awareness where it could continue to wreak havoc in our lives.

This awareness is such an important part of the healing process, because no matter how powerful the therapies we use to quell the symptoms. If we don't also acknowledge and address the real sources of our stress, then we'll probably keep finding ourselves faced with the same situations over and over again.

Relieve Stress, Anxiety, Burnout, Panic Attacks & Agoraphobia
The Same Way I Did

So I'm sure you are wondering how, with all this confusion, you are supposed to get to the root of the problem, or to identify the real contributing factors or causes of your stress. But before we get to that let's take a look at some of the most common causes, and at some examples as to why it can be so difficult to identify them.

Some of the causes of stress include:

A sudden or unexpected event which could literally cause a shock to the system.

An ongoing or underlying negative problem which you may or may not have identified as being a source of stress.

Poor life style

Poor or under developed life skills

When stress, anxiety or panic attacks are a result of an unexpected or tragic event, it can be devastating. Examples of this could include: the loss of a loved one, a diagnosis of a terminal illness, a loss of a job or status, an injury or accident, or some sort of shocking news. Many people who experience this type of event, may even be thrown into a state of depression.

www.stressawarenessandprevention.com
www.thementalwellnessrevolution.com

When faced with these types of life altering events there is usually a natural grieving process. However, if the intensity of the situation is severe enough that it literally feels more like a shock to the system, it will likely take much longer for a person to move through it. When stress is a result of such an experience or a tragic loss, and if the symptoms are acute enough, as in you are experiencing intense physical, mental and emotional distress, you may even end up suffering with a condition called Post Traumatic Stress Disorder.

At times like this the first thing I'd suggest that you do is to surround yourself with as much support as possible. You may find this support in family or friends or you may also want to seek the advice of your doctor. He or she might refer you to a psychologist or may even prescribe medication to help you to deal with the loss or grief. When you feel the time is right you may also want to find someone who is trained in a therapy such as TFT as it has proven to be very powerful for helping to relieve symptoms from trauma.

If on the other hand your stress is a result of some sort of ongoing underlying issue, that you may, or may not have even identified as being a source of stress, you may still suffer the effects. Some examples of this could be when someone is having financial difficulties, someone who is lonely and feeling disconnected from their community, or someone who feels trapped in a situation such as an abusive relationship or poor working conditions. Very often we are aware of what caused the stress but it may seem as though we have no choice in the matter, or means to change our situation.

As I mentioned earlier one of the reasons this happens is because it is not always obvious how a particular problem (such as having financial difficulties) can have such a negative impact on how we feel (such as suffering the physical symptoms of stress), or our lives in general. So consequently we may be very aware that we are stressed but we unwittingly blame the wrong issue as being the cause. Here are a few examples of how this can happen.

After I had recovered from my anxiety and panic attacks I was coaching a client who was as stressed and anxious as I had been during the height of my ordeal with the condition. She was also suffering from panic attacks and other than leaving her home to go to work she was all but housebound. I could certainly identify with what she was going through.

As we were discussing her stress and what she thought had caused it, she told me that it had been brought on by her home life. This included issues such as: dealing with the pressures of having to find reliable daycare for her child, the guilt she felt for having to ask her aging mother to help look after her son, and the constant arguments she was having with her husband. These run-ins between the couple were usually about her not being home when her son finished school, the family seldom eating meals together, and the lack of family time. At first glance, and according to her it appeared that the problems were all stemming from the relationship between her and her husband, and around family time. Things were so bad that they had even talked about a divorce.

However when I asked this client about her work, she immediately assured me that she loved her job and that it had been the only stable thing in her life, for many years. She kept telling me that her employers really needed her and that they depended on her so much that she just couldn't let them down.

I wanted some more information so I asked her what she specifically liked about this job. Much to her surprise, her answer immediately revealed that she didn't particularly like the job at all. The work was not at all rewarding, and she had to put in very long hours. On top of that she had agreed to a pay cut several years back due to a turn in the economy, for which she still hadn't been compensated for even though it had picked up again. As she was telling me this I could see a shift in her whole demeanor. It was as if she had for the first time become aware of how she really felt about her job and the problems that it was contributing to in her life.

This awareness also helped her realize that the cut in pay had left her feeling very vulnerable, and consequently she had been fearful of losing her job ever since. And that it had been this fear that had kept her stuck there all along.

All of a sudden she sat up straight in her chair, the colour came back to her face and she was able to breathe much easier. Without realizing it, she had stopped trembling and shifted out of a state of stress and into a state of relief and relaxation. The interesting thing was that it wasn't until she actually said any of this out loud that she even realized how she felt about her job or how it was affecting her life. Because she had spent so many years convincing herself that she liked and needed the job, she hadn't ever really stopped to think about how it was affecting her personal life or her relationship with her husband.

For her, because she was focussing on all of the problems which had stemmed from the fact that she was working in this job, being the daycare and family issues, she had failed to see that it was the job itself. And her beliefs and fears around letting these people down that was actually keeping her stuck. And although she had suffered with this debilitating stress and anxiety for several years, the mere fact that we had now pinpointed what was really causing it turned out to be enough for her to experience some immediate relief.

Since she was financially able to quit her job the next thing we did was discuss her options, and I coached her on how best to negotiate a better agreement. This coaching session was enough to help her realize what was really causing her stress, and in turn this awareness put her in a position to resolve her own problem. This alone was enough to literally lift a weight, or the burden off her shoulders, and her anxiety literally disappeared in that moment in time. It was like watching an immediate transformation and she walked out of the session a very different person to what she was when she walked in.

Now I realize that not everyone in this sort of situation will be in the position to just quit their job. However, having this sort of awareness will put you in a more powerful and resourceful position, and allow you to start generating some alternative plans.

To be honest my own experience with stress manifested in a similar way to this clients, that being that I was not really aware of what had caused it. Only for me I was blaming my job while failing to realize that the reason I remained working there was because of my partner. And the fact that he was so insecure about me pursuing my own career goals.

Yes, I hated the job, I found it boring and unrewarding, and since I had been used to having a lot of control over my own life I found the job to be stifling. So I blamed the job for the stress and dissatisfaction in my life. And although it is true that the job was a major contributing factor to my unhappiness and stress, the real underlying cause of it, and reason that I was working for someone else in the first place, was because of my now "ex".

So as you can see I too had originally failed to see the underlying source, or contributing factors to my stress. However upon realizing what had really caused it, I was then faced with a whole new set of problems. Those being that in order to resolve this issue, I would have either needed some cooperation and support from my partner, or I could have been putting my relationship in jeopardy. Herein lays a huge problem that keeps so many people stuck in all sorts of unhealthy situations, sometimes for many years.

When stress has been brought on by a relationship of any sort, be it personal, romantic or professional. And where there is a threat or fear of losing the security of that relationship, we often find ourselves faced with a whole new set of challenges. And it may be these challenges in themselves that turn out to be the real underlying cause of stress.

This is particularly evident where there are strong emotions involved, especially if it means there is a threat of having to end the relationship in order to resolve the problem which is causing the stress. This whole issue can become very complicated and the stress may be compounded by the fear of losing something that has become so familiar in your life. Under these circumstances, it can actually become very difficult for a person to even admit to what is really causing their stress, even though deep down inside they are very aware of its cause.

I'm sure that you can see in both of the examples how easy it can be to get sidetracked from the real cause of stress. We can actually become so consumed by the stress itself, or with the problems that have been created by it, that we end up missing or ignoring the warning signs. Consequently when this happens we may end up never dealing with whatever it was that created the stress in the first place. But instead, we try to ignore it until something activates it again.

This cycle may then go on and on until it either reaches a breaking point, or where the person cracks. Or, the problem may get to be so big and overwhelming that it may seem that the only way to resolve it would be for the person to remove themselves from the situation altogether.

My point here though is about the lack of awareness, or the willingness to see where the real stress in your life is coming from. As while so many people fail to recognize the real causes of stress, or worse yet "defend their position" as to why they think they are stressed. These underlying sources of conflict have the power to become immobilizing, and they can keep a person stuck for years. Sadly, as uncomfortable as this lack of awareness may be, it is not that uncommon at all.

The same can be said for someone who feels stuck in a job which they don't like because they have to depend on the income and are too afraid to leave. This keeps people stuck in jobs which they hate and which suck the life out of them for years. I hear and see this sort of thing all of the time, and the more desperate we feel, the less choice it may seem that we have.

Another area where people experience stress in their lives as a result of this lack of awareness, is when a person knows that he or she is not happy with his or her life, or with a part of it, but they have no idea of what it is that they want instead. As crazy as this may sound this is a major source of stress, and it is the "rut" that millions of people find themselves "stuck in" every single day.

This is an issue that causes literally millions of men and women to live a great deal of their lives in turmoil. Yet, as impossible as it may seem to figure out what they want, with the right tools it is easy to start uncovering you true passions and purpose in life. To get started on the process you can go to my website www.suzanneprice.com and download a free coaching tool which I created called The Triple AAA Coaching Tool. It's my gift to you so please do take advantage of that.

www.stressawarenessandprevention.com
www.thementalwellnessrevolution.com

I have written a book and workshop called Its Your Life - So What Are You Going To Do With It? I love teaching and coaching people around this topic because it is possible to experience some major shifts in your life and to start living the life you were meant to live.

The point that I'm trying to make here is that this awareness is the key to being able to recognize what choices we really do have in our lives. It also allows us to come up with some possible solutions to our problems.

If you want to make positive change in your life you must first decide to live life as consciously as possible so that you can become clear about what it is that you want or need to change. As it is only then that you'll ever be able to create a master plan and break it down in steps to make it manageable enough to achieve.

Following is a list of some of the issues that cause people to become stressed. By recognizing which areas are problematic in your own life will give you the power to make some positive changes.

Money And Financial Issues

Loneliness And Lack Of Connection

Disconnect From Community

A Lack Of Family Support Or Partnership With A Significant Other

Career

Relationships

Lack Of Friends

Weak Social Or Family Structure

Health Issues

Bad Habits

Monumental Events Such As Family Rituals Including Birthdays And Seasonal Holidays Like Christmas

School Or University

Unsupportive Living Or Working Environment

Boredom

Feeling That You Have No Power Or Control Over Your Life

Feeling Trapped In A Situation That You Cannot Leave

www.stressawarenessandprevention.com
www.thementalwellnessrevolution.com

Lack Of Self Awareness

Poor Spiritual Connection

Feeling Helpless Or Hopeless

Feeling Stuck In A Rut.

Don't forget that if you are feeling stuck in a certain area of your life, or if you are feeling stuck in life in general you can change this. Start by going to my website www.suzanneprice.com and download The Triple AAA Coaching Tool. This is a powerful tool which I designed to help you start finding some clarity in your life.

Reinvent Yourself To Become A More Confident And Empowered Version of You!

As I mentioned earlier, whenever someone has suffered with something as debilitating as anxiety, panic attacks or depression, it is not uncommon for him or her to take on the belief that they are no longer capable of doing the things they used to do. Some may fall for the lie that this is now just a part of who, he or she is. Or, they may even convince themselves that they are no longer the person that they used to be.

These new beliefs, which are typically very negative or at least limiting, often become part of an individual's new reality. They become ingrained into a person's mind, and attached to their identity. When this happens it is not uncommon for a person to unconsciously commit to living their life within the limitations that have now seeped into his or her subconscious mind. And will likely prevent this person from even being able to imagine feeling any other way. This is especially so for anyone who has suffered with such a life altering condition for a prolonged period of time.

Relieve Stress, Anxiety, Burnout, Panic Attacks & Agoraphobia The Same Way I Did

What this then means is that no matter how desperately that person might want to rid themselves of these emotional shackles, they may feel as though they just cannot set themselves free. This is especially so for anyone who is unable to recall a time when they were not suffering with the condition, although such powerful beliefs can have the same impact on those who had previously experienced a happier, healthier life.

The point being, that it is often the beliefs that anchor, or weigh a person down, keeping them stuck and preventing them from moving forward. And this is in part due to the fact that it can often be difficult to identify which beliefs, are responsible for ruining our lives. However until we can uncover them, we may feel as though we are spinning our wheels and become extremely frustrated, not to mention desperate to break free.

I knew this experience well. It hadn't taken long before I started to realize that I was no longer really living my life. In fact it felt more as though I was merely existing. Logically, nothing made sense, and since I'd never suffered with anything like this before you'd think that I should have been able to recover quite quickly. I was desperate to get well, and I was trying everything that I could to overcome it. But as crazy as it sounds, it really did feel as though there was some invisible force holding me back.

Physically I had been immobilized by fear, and mentally and emotionally incapacitated by the desperate frustration of not being able to get beyond this. My anxiety and panic attacks had been so debilitating at one point, that I now also had the evidence of what might happen if I ever tried to push myself too far. This had all contributed to me developing some very limiting beliefs of what I felt that I was now capable, or incapable of doing. I had gotten to the point where I was literally living within the confines of my own fears and limiting beliefs, and yet I was desperate to escape them.

I often likened my situation as having had a curse put on me which I just couldn't break free of. I was desperate, frustrated and tired. And even though I had made some progress with the symptoms, and was determined to get well, there were times when I had to resign myself to the fact that I'd probably never overcome this.

I often felt doomed, and like so many others, I sometime felt like giving up. However, I'd soon be reminded of the fact that I really didn't have anything left, to give up. I'd already made so many compromises in my life and I had had to lower my expectations of myself so many times that I literally had nothing else to give. This often made me feel worse as it seemed as though I had ran out of bargaining chips. I sometimes wondered if my life at the time was as good as it was going to get.

Then one day when I was beating myself up for not being able to get out of this rut, and while thinking about how my fears had been preventing me from doing all of the things that I loved to do. I had a bit of an epiphany. I was thinking about all of the things that I was fearful of, and trying to figure out where in my life, that the fear was not holding me back. This made me aware of the fact that this fear was literally holding me back from living the life that I had dreamed of. And since I'd never really thought too much of dying, or the fear of dying, it suddenly dawned on me that it was now as if I was living my life as though I was actually more afraid of living, than I was of dying. Or at least, afraid of living the life that I desperately wanted to live.

This made me feel quite angry. I was angry at the fear and the fact that it was controlling my entire life. For the longest time I had been pleading with the fear to just let me have my life back, and at the time I was willing to do anything in order to have this happen. In fact I'd made so many compromises it felt as though I'd been making a deal with the devil.

I also became really frustrated, because even though I had done so much to try to get over this I still wasn't able to. And this anger and frustration seemed to push me to a point where I decided that I was no longer willing to do this. I was no longer willing to settle for having my old life back either, because even though I thought that I'd been pretty independent and free spirited. I had still been holding back in some areas. I had always been afraid to say what I really wanted to say, do what I wanted to do, or face some of my fears. And now I'd had enough. What this meant was that now I wanted to change all of this.

I'd had enough of all of this crap in my life and I wasn't willing to compromise in the same way any longer. I decided that I wanted to be more confident, more courageous and more outgoing. I wasn't willing to take the back seat, to sit still, to shut up and be quiet, or to give up on my own dreams. Now I decided that I wanted become unstoppable, and that nobody was going to tell me any different. And since I'd been saying this to the therapists all along, and they'd been responding by telling me that I just needed to accept myself for who I was. I realized that I had to go this alone.

I was no longer willing to listen to people who wanted to tell me who I was supposed to be, how I was supposed to feel, what I was supposed to do, or how I was supposed to live my life. From here on I decided that it was time to start following my own heart, and to break free from the limitations of my old life.

What this meant was, that I now knew that I had to completely reinvent myself. This was probably the first time in my life that I really felt as though I had the power to take my life into my own hands, and to take control of my future. And although it is believed that depression is a symptom of what is lost in the past, and anxiety is a fear of the unknown, or the future. I personally believe that both are driven by elements of control, or lack of. As in, these conditions have their roots firmly attached to fears of being controlled, or not having enough control over our own lives.

Ultimately, anxiety, panic attacks, depression and most other so called "mental illnesses" are affected by a lack of freedom and choice we have in our lives. As well as, the feeling of disconnect which so many people now experience, with that being, a feeling of disconnect from ourselves, others, our true passions, the purpose of our own lives, and community.

www.stressawarenessandprevention.com
www.thementalwellnessrevolution.com

With that said, it is very likely that besides wanting to rid ourselves of anxiety, panic attacks, depression, or what have you, that most people also want to make positive changes in their lives. Most people are dissatisfied with their life, or at least with specific parts of it. However the problem is that the majority of these people do not even know what they want instead. Or, could it be that they are simply unaware of what could be possible.

This is actually one of the biggest causes of stress, anxiety and depression in so many people's lives, and is the reason why I am so passionate about helping people discover what they want. In fact I've written a book and teach a workshop called It's Your Life – So What Are You Going To Do With It? With that said it is time for you to start working on the next piece of the puzzle.

While working through the following exercises you might want to go onto my website www.suzanneprice.com and download the free coaching tool called The Triple AAA Coaching Formulae. I've designed it to help you start figuring out what you want to do with your life, and where you want to make positive changes.

www.stressawarenessandprevention.com
www.thementalwellnessrevolution.com

Reinvent Yourself, Your Life, And Your Future

One of the problems we encounter when we are unhappy with a part of our life, or with life in general, is that this unhappiness can be all encompassing. As a result we then unconsciously put so much of our awareness, attention and energy on these particular areas, and the thoughts and feelings which are generated by them, that, it can be very difficult to even think about what we want instead. And until we can shift our attention onto what we want, it may be all but impossible to bring about positive change. With that said, let's start creating a vision about who you want to become and how you want to live your life in the future.

Creating A Master Plan Of How You Would See A More Empowered Version Of Yourself And Your Future Life

In order to create the changes that you would like to experience in your life you must first consider the possibilities. Then you will need to create a master plan, or a vision, of what you would like your future self, and life to look like. Now I know that if you have faced a lot of challenges, or have experienced a lot of fear or self-doubt in your life, you may wonder, what is the point? Also, you may instinctively want to discard this idea right away, but I urge you not to do that. In fact, I encourage you to try working with the following tips and tools.

I'm sure at this point you are batting around all sorts of negative thoughts in your head and reasons as to why you shouldn't even waste your time. You may be thinking things like: I'll never be able to live the life I want to live; this is just the way I am and I'll never be able to change; I don't have the money, or education, courage or support to be able to achieve this sort of change; or I'm too scared, not good enough or don't deserve the life I dream of. Or you may even be thinking about what others might think about you, or say, if you did make the changes you desire, or wonder about whom in your life may disapprove. Scarier yet, there could even be a risk of having to give something, or someone up in the process, because let's face it, it is not uncommon for others to feel threatened when we change.

There are potentially hundreds if not thousands of negative thoughts that could be trying to sabotage you right now, and they may even be preventing you from creating this vision. Just as importantly, you may also have some very real obstacles that have been getting in your way, such as not having enough money or the means to make some of these changes right now. Even so, these obstacles, objections and saboteurs are no excuse for you not to do this exercise. Hey, it's just an exercise after all, albeit a very powerful one so just do it. If done with an open heart and mind, it really could help you to expand your capacity to think outside of your own, "box, which is quite likely pretty small at the moment. Not to mention overflowing with all sorts of crud.

With that said, I'm going to suggest that you imagine having somewhere to store all of these negative thoughts for the time being, just so that you have a way of physically separating them. Perhaps you could imagine having a separate box, or a shelf, or even cloud in the sky where you can place all of those negative thoughts and feelings. You need somewhere where you can leave them for safe keeping, or at least for the time being. Then, if you notice any of these saboteurs trying to interrupt your train of thought by popping into your head uninvited, you can simply visualize yourself putting them in that allocated space where they now belong. This of course being the box, shelf, or cloud, whichever one you decided to place them in earlier.

www.stressawarenessandprevention.com
www.thementalwellnessrevolution.com

This process will allow you to have the mental and emotional space needed to think freely, and to be creative. Now all you have to do is create a vision of the person whom you would love to become in the future, and the life that you would love to live

This project is a huge part of the healing process, because a well defined vision will allow you to see what could be possible in your life. And it will serve as a motivational superpower. It will become a tool that can help pull you out of the crud which has been holding you down for so long. With that said, it is important that you make this vision as clear, and as enticing as possible, and to do so you will need to tap into your creative and sensory powers.

What this means is that you are going to use all of your senses to make this vision as real and as positive, and empowering as you could possibly imagine. Since you want to create a picture of the ideal or perfect life, start by asking yourself these following questions. In a perfect world, if I could become anyone or anything I desire, and succeed at creating my dream life, if only in a picture, who would I become and what would this life look like?

Since you'll want to make this vision to be as sensory as possible, ask yourself the following question. How would it feel, to step into that life, even if it were only for a moment? How could this experience change the life that I am presently living today, and the way I feel right now?

Following are some examples of questions that you might want to consider in order to illicit the thoughts and feeling that will assist you in creating your vision. This vision will become the template of the master plan for your future empowered life.

Future Empowered Identity Of Self

Let's take this one step at the time. I'm going to start by helping you create a vision of a more empowered version of yourself.

What about yourself (personal being) would you like to experience differently? How would you like to feel? What would this change look like? Consider things like your image, posture, how you move, breathe or interact with others. How much energy will you have? What about your facial expressions? How would others see you? How much more comfortable would you be when interacting with other people. How would this affect your personal, professional or social life? How confident will you look and feel?

www.stressawarenessandprevention.com
www.thementalwellnessrevolution.com

Will this new and improved, and more confident version of yourself take more chances, travel more, or choose a different path in life? Notice how you might carry yourself differently. Think about how you might feel or what you might think about yourself. What sort of things might you say to yourself? Consider all of the ways you could become more confident and empowered, and start writing a list of them.

Create A Vision Of A More Empowered Life

Now that you have spent some time thinking about how you would like to reinvent yourself, think about how you would like to live your life from here on. How would you like to spend your time? As you consider the possibilities of becoming more confident and empowered, also think about how this could positively affect your life.

Consider some of the things that you have thought about doing, but have not done yet because fear has gotten in your way. If you were fearless, unstoppable, empowered or confident, what new things might you want to try now? Are there any new activities that you would like to do? By making these positive changes and by challenging yourself, how would your health, wellbeing and happiness be improved? Who else in your life would benefit from your new level of confidence and energy? Notice all of the things that you would like better about yourself if you had more confidence. Think about all of the ways your life might improve as a result of having more confidence, and keep adding these positive ideas to your list.

Is there a word or a statement that really speaks to you, and that would keep you inspired and motivated enough to bring this positive change into your life? For instance I reached a point where I decided that I wanted to become UNSTOPABLE! What about you, you may not have one yet but start listening out for those messages that your subconscious is trying to get you to pay attention to. The positive and empowering ones!

Next, using these as well as any other questions or ideas you may already have, or that may come up for you in the future, start creating a vision. Build it around the version of yourself that you would like to become, or around the life you would like to live.

Make this vision as clear and detailed and inspiring and as sensory rich as possible. Remember to think about how you may feel, what you may see, hear, taste or smell differently when living a more sensory rich life. You may even have intuitive thoughts and feelings that are trying to get your attention as well.

If you are a visual person you may even want to create a collage or vision board. If you would rather write, then maybe start a journal or write in a planner, whichever one works best for you. Although in saying that, I'm going to suggest that you write with ink on paper as opposed to using a computer or tablet. Get these thoughts and feelings into your mind body system, or muscle memory. And keep focusing on how your life could be better as a result of overcoming these limiting beliefs, and reinventing yourself. Just start brainstorming now!

When you are ready you can gather all of this information, and start creating a fantastic vision of your ultimate goal. Make it as positive and enticing as possible. Run through all of the positive scenarios in your mind and then fantasize about how life could be different in as many ways possible. Be sure to only focus on the positive.

When you have finished gathering all of this information, write a statement about what you want to achieve and how you are going to achieve it.

When you have finished this exercise, start thinking about how you will go about breaking this vision down into a set of goals. Then make a list of steps that you will need to take to achieve them, as each step will then become a mini goal. From here you can start taking action, and will start to move yourself forward, and towards making positive changes in your life.

This is an ongoing process, meaning that you can keep adding to it on a daily basis. Whenever you experience a setback or feel overwhelmed, which you will from time to time (that's just human nature), put those negative thoughts into the space you allocated for them earlier. Then get back on track by thinking about the possibilities of how you could change your life, and how you might be able to resolve the things that are bothering you.

If you are interested in getting some help around how to create your life's master plan, you might want to check out my coaching program and upcoming book called its Your Life – So What Are You Going To Do With It?

www.stressawarenessandprevention.com
www.thementalwellnessrevolution.com

Creating A Powerful Version Of Yourself - Visualization Exercise

To help you with this amazing exercise, pull out the list which you have been creating which includes all of the changes you would like to make in your life, and the vision of the person you would like to become.

Next, select a few of the personal characteristics or qualities that you'd like to incorporate into your personal identity. Perhaps they would include qualities such as to be confident, happy, outgoing, self-assured, accepting of others and assertive.

Think about what these things really mean to you, and ponder them for a few minutes. Consider how a person with these qualities would act, behave, carry themselves, interact with others, or think and feel. Imagine how you would feel if you were able to take on some of these characteristics.

When you feel as though you have a good grasp of how this change would positively impact *your* life. And you are clear about which aspects you would definitely like to enhance or incorporate into your personal identity, or life, first, then do the following exercise.

Visualization Exercise

It is dusk and you are standing under a street lamp when you notice someone walking towards you. This person is confident, reassured, and looks as though they really "have it together. They have the very characteristics that you would love to enhance, or incorporate into your own new empowered version of yourself (insert your own descriptive words here, select them from the list of qualities that you just generated).

This person is someone who you admire, who inspires you, and who you aspire to be like. Looking diligently you can tell that this person has all of the qualities and characteristics that you would love experience.

In the darkness, you cannot see who this person is but you sense a certain familiarity. Struggling to see who is walking towards you, you sense a certain excitement, and feel at ease with their presence.

That stranger moving towards you is somehow giving you strength, hope and a sense of power. As they approach, you feel more confident, empowered and alive. You feel their positive energy just by being in their presence and you feel it washing over you.

www.stressawarenessandprevention.com
www.thementalwellnessrevolution.com

Now as this person gets closer, you notice that he or she is really happy, content and confident, and is the person that you would love to be.

You feel their happiness and contentment too. In fact they have such great energy that you feel energized by them and empowered by their presence. You haven't felt this good in a long time, so you take a really deep breath and feel their protection. The feeling is almost overwhelming.

Then, as he or she steps forward into the light which is now shining down on them as well yourself, you can see their face.

You take another deep breath as you feel yourself being drawn into their energy. As you step towards this incredible person, your whole being is so happy to see him/her. With a feeling of happiness, joy and pride, you let out a huge sigh of relief as you realize that this perfect stranger is in fact....
YOU!

Take a moment to connect with this vision and savour these feelings of your success.

Ask your subconscious mind to accept and integrate these positive changes into your entire being.

Relieve Stress, Anxiety, Burnout, Panic Attacks & Agoraphobia
The Same Way I Did

As you are doing this visualization, be sure to take the characteristics from the list you generated earlier, and integrate them into your mind body system by attaching them to the person in this visualization.

You can repeat this exercise frequently by adding more powerful emotional resources each time you do it. Also see yourself getting closer and closer to the vision of the stranger, until you eventually become at one with them.

Take pride in knowing that you are now taking the steps towards positive change in your life. Just by recognizing and admitting what you want to achieve in life, you have started the process of becoming that person which you desire to be.

You can gain confidence, you can gain strength, you can change the way you look, and feel, as well as how you respond and relate to others. You can live the life you want to live. We are all constantly reinventing ourselves throughout our lives, so why not chose to do it consciously. By doing so you will be able to become the person you really want to be, and live the life you want to live. Why not become the best version of yourself possible?

www.stressawarenessandprevention.com
www.thementalwellnessrevolution.com

Waking Up To A Better Day

This exercise is a great supplement to the visualization you just did. It should help you generate some ideas, and hopefully inspire you to take steps towards becoming a more empowered version of yourself.

Sometimes when we are stressed, anxious or depressed the mere thought of getting out of bed and facing the day can be challenging enough. This may be especially so if we find ourselves waking up feeling as though we are about to face yet another day of doom and gloom.

I know this feeling well since I'd spent the best part of ten years living within the limits of my anxiety. A condition that had pushed me to the point that I was so filled with doubt about ever getting beyond it, that I couldn't even imagine my life being any other way. Then one day in an effort to distract myself from all of the scary thoughts I started to visualize, dreaming about beautiful places around the world. I then thought about activities that looked as though they would be fun, and finally about things that I would like to try doing myself. The more I did this the better I became at creating new movies in my mind, and I finally started to see the possibilities, and the process evolved from there.

This is actually a very powerful process, so I'm going to suggest that you do it regardless of how you feel, and that you do it every single day. The best time to work through this process is as soon as you wake up in the morning, before you even get out of bed.

Start by making yourself as comfortable as possible. Then simply ask yourself the following question. If I could spend the day doing anything my heart desired, what would that be? Then just relax and let your subconscious mind generate some ideas. Allow your mind to wonder and dream about how you would ideally spend your day?

Don't worry if you come up blank and nothing comes to mind. Most people when stressed, anxious or depressed have no idea what they want, and that is often part of the reason why they feel so awful to begin with. If you can't come up with any good ideas today, then simply try asking yourself the same question tomorrow, and the next day, and so on. And if you still can't think of what you would like to be doing with your day, or how you would like to be spending your time, then try thinking about someone who is already living the kind of life that you would like to live. This person may be someone you know, or even a character on a television show, perhaps someone who inspires you, or who participates in an activity that you would like to try.

Also, if when you ask yourself this question, your mind starts bombarding you with all sorts of reasons why you couldn't possibly live any other way, then just set those thoughts aside. Remember to put them in that special space you allocated for them in the last exercise. The box, shelf or cloud, or where ever it was that you decided to store your negative thoughts, limiting beliefs, obstacles and objections.

Then ask yourself the same question again. You might even want to reframe the question by asking yourself to, just imagine, even for just one minute, what it is that you would love to be doing with your time. Or, if you were able to remove the obstacles that have gotten in your way in the past, what would you do? How would you be living differently as a happy person?

Most people at some point in their lives feel stuck. They know that they are not happy with their life, but they don't know what they want instead.

www.stressawarenessandprevention.com
www.thementalwellnessrevolution.com

Anxious and depressed people often feel very stuck, and even if they do know what they want, they often feel that it is just not possible to have, or achieve it. Some people have felt stuck for so long that they may actually feel defeated, or even doomed. However you must hang in there, be patient and persistent. I know this can be very hard to do if you've already suffered for a long time, but things can change for the better.

Just remember that the whole point of doing this exercise is to shake up the crud in your mind so that you can start generating some fresh new ideas. You need to start stretching the boundaries of your present reality, and this is true even if it means that you start by expanding whatever is currently within your own mind.

At this point you do not have to do anything with any of the ideas that come to mind. It is simply an exercise that will help you tap into your creative brain, and will eventually help you see more choice and possibilities.

Then when you have finished your little brain storming session, and while still lying down, stretch. Stretch out all of your muscles and take a few good breaths. Sit up and stretch your arms high up into the air, then out to the sides and then out in front of you. Wiggle your fingers, clench your fists and then release them, shake your hands and arms out. Stretch your legs, wiggle your toes, and rotate your ankles. Stretch your arms up again and take a big deep breath. Then get up and stretch again. Drink some fresh water and take a shower, get dressed and get ready for the day. Make the effort to look and feel your best even if you don't have anything planned or you don't think it's worth it.

I have always found that a shower can be very invigorating, and suggest that you start with nice warm water to soothe tense muscles. Then, gradually cool the water down so that you end with a nice cool rinse, this will really wake you up.

When I was suffering with anxiety, panic attacks and depression I found that taking a shower was a great way to change my state, which ultimately helped me to feel better. I also noticed that I was able to think more clearly, and allowed me to have some major mental breakthroughs.

What I had not realized until recently, and this is actually quite fascinating, is that we are usually more grounded, and connected to the earth when we are standing in the shower. This can have a huge impact on how you think and feel. So don't overlook the importance of this idea. One of the only other times that you will ever feel this grounded is when you are walking barefoot on a sandy beach.

Final Word

As I mentioned before, the exercises that I have presented in this book are similar to the ones that helped me overcome my own debilitating experience with stress, anxiety, panic attacks, burnout and agoraphobia. I say similar, because when I started experimenting with the different therapies, I was still learning how to use them. None of which had been developed specifically for the purpose of helping with such a condition, so overtime I have adapted some of them to make them more relevant.

At the time that I was going through this, I had become aware that there were many aspects to suffering with this condition, and that each aspect needed to be dealt with in a different way. And knowing that I was able to see how the different modalities worked, or how different exercises within the modalities could possibly help to alleviate some of the different aspects, I was able to customize my own healing.

This for me was a journey of trial and error which took place over a number of years. However, now that I have tweaked the whole program and only included the exercises that are, in my opinion the most powerful, I am able to present it to you in a much more complete state. I only wish that I had had such a user friendly program available to me when I was trying to get well.

When I say that I know how debilitating such a condition can be, you can take comfort in knowing that I truly do. I also know how stubborn and relentless it can be to try and overcome it, but you have to believe that you can conquer this. It may not happen overnight, and you may sometimes feel like there is no other way than to limit your lifestyle in order to avoid the discomfort. While it is ok to do that from time to time, I want to encourage you to keep trying. Slowly but surely, if you commit to making the necessary changes in your life, and learn the tools which can help to manage the symptoms, you will increase your odds of not only surviving this, but in thriving in the future as well.

I wish you well on your journey to recovery. Please don't forget to check out the websites which I've listed below to download some free tools, and to sign up for the newsletter. This is the best way to learn about any upcoming events, or new tools that I'll be launching in the near future.

Wishing you peace, love, health and happiness,

Suzanne

www.suzanneprice.com

www.stressawarenessandprevention.com

www.thementalwellnessrevolution.com

www.stressawarenessandprevention.com
www.thementalwellnessrevolution.com

NOTES

www.stressawarenessandprevention.com
www.thementalwellnessrevolution.com

NOTES

www.stressawarenessandprevention.com
www.thementalwellnessrevolution.com

NOTES

www.stressawarenessandprevention.com
www.thementalwellnessrevolution.com

NOTES

www.ingramcontent.com/pod-product-compliance
Lightning Source LLC
Chambersburg PA
CBHW070809100426
42742CB00012B/2305